WORDPRESS FOR LIBRARIES

Library Technology Essentials

About the Series

The *Library Technology Essentials* series helps librarians utilize today's hottest new technologies as well as ready themselves for tomorrow's. The series features titles that cover the A–Z of how to leverage the latest and most cutting-edge technologies and trends to deliver new library services.

Today's forward-thinking libraries are responding to changes in information consumption, new technological advancements, and growing user expectations by devising groundbreaking ways to remain relevant in a rapidly changing digital world. This collection of primers guides libraries along the path to innovation through step-by-step instruction. Written by the field's top experts, these handbooks serve as the ultimate gateway to the newest and most promising emerging technology trends. Filled with practical advice and projects for libraries to implement right now, these books inspire readers to start leveraging these new techniques and tools today.

About the Series Editor

Ellyssa Kroski is the Director of Information Technology at the New York Law Institute as well as an award-winning editor and author of 22 books including *Law Librarianship in the Digital Age* for which she won the AALL's 2014 Joseph L. Andrews Legal Literature Award. Her ten-book technology series, The Tech Set, won the ALA's Best Book in Library Literature Award in 2011. She is a librarian, an adjunct faculty member at Pratt Institute, and an international conference speaker. She speaks at several conferences a year, mainly about new tech trends, digital strategy, and libraries.

Titles in the Series

WORDPRESS FOR LIBRARIES

Chad Haefele

ROWMAN & LITTLEFIELD
Lanham • Boulder • New York • London

Published by Rowman & Littlefield
A wholly owned subsidary of The Rowman & Littlefield Publishing Group,
Inc.
4501 Forbes Boulevard, Suite 200, Lanham, Maryland 20706
www.rowman.com

Unit A, Whitacre Mews, 26-34 Stannary Street, London SE11 4AB

British Library Cataloguing in Publication Information Available

Library of Congress Cataloging-in-Publication Data

Haefele, Chad, 1982-
WordPress for libraries / Chad Haefele.
pages cm — (Library technology essentials ; 6)
Includes bibliographical references and index.
ISBN 978-1-4422-5305-6 (cloth : alk. paper) — ISBN 978-1-4422-5306-3 (pbk. : alk. paper) —
ISBN 978-1-4422-5307-0 (ebook)
1. Library Web sites—Design. 2. WordPress (Electronic resource) 3. Blogs—Computer programs.
4. Web sites—Authoring programs. I. Title.
Z674.75.W67H34 2015
025.0422—dc23
2015011514

♾ ™ The paper used in this publication meets the minimum requirements of
American National Standard for Information Sciences Permanence of Paper
for Printed Library Materials, ANSI/NISO Z39.48-1992.

Printed in the United States of America

For Melissa, Nora, and all the colleagues who helped
me learn about WordPress

CONTENTS

SERIES EDITOR'S FOREWORD

WordPress for Libraries is a complete how-to handbook that provides practical tips and best practices for creating an engaging library website using WordPress. This outstanding work informs readers about everything from hosting options and installation instructions, to how to gather traffic statistics and set up security for a library's website. Follow along with WordPress expert Chad Haefele as he leads readers through how to install and use plugins and themes, how to create their own child themes and shortcodes, how to build a professional library website, how to create an online exhibit to display image collections, and more. This outstanding book is chock-full of invaluable advice and recommendations for establishing an exceptional web presence for your library using WordPress.

The idea for the Library Technology Essentials book series came about because there have been many drastic changes in information consumption, new technological advancements, and growing user expectations over the past few years, all of which forward thinking libraries are responding to by devising groundbreaking ways to remain relevant in a rapidly changing digital world. I saw a need for a practical set of guidebooks which libraries could use to inform themselves about how to stay on the cutting edge by implementing new programs, services, and technologies to match their patrons' expectations.

Libraries today are embracing new and emerging technologies, transforming themselves into community hubs and places of cocreation through makerspaces, developing information commons spaces, and even taking on new roles and formats, all the while searching for ways to decrease budget lines, add value, and prove the ROI of the library. The Library Technology Essentials series is a collection of primers to guide libraries along the path to innovation through step-by-step instruction. Written by the field's top experts, these handbooks are meant to serve as the ultimate gateway to the newest and most promising emerging technology trends. Filled with practical advice and project ideas for libraries to implement right now, these books will hopefully inspire readers to start leveraging these new techniques and tools today.

Each book follows the same format and outline, guiding the reader through the A–Z of how to leverage the latest and most cutting-edge technologies and trends to deliver new library services. Chapter 5, the "Projects" chapter, comprises the largest portion of the book, providing library initiatives that can be implemented by both beginner and advanced readers accommodating for all audiences and levels of technical expertise. These projects and programs range from the basic "How to Circulate Wearable Technology in Your Library" and "How to Host a FIRST Robotics Team at the Library," to intermediate such as "How to Create a Hands-Free Digital Exhibit Showcase with Microsoft Kinect," to the more advanced options such as "Implementing a Scalable E-Resources Management System" and "How to Gamify Library Orientation for Patrons with a Top Down Video Game." Readers of all skill levels will find something of interest in these books.

After finding Haefele's online presentation on "Rock Your Library's Content with WordPress" which discusses the strengths and scalability of WordPress for library applications I knew that he was the perfect choice to author this book. As the emerging technologies librarian at University of North Carolina (UNC) at Chapel Hill for the past eight years, Haefele helped bring UNC's large university library website to the next level by implementing the WordPress content management system. And after working with him and reading his finished manuscript, I can definitely say that the folks at *Library Journal* chose well when they named him a 2011 Mover and Shaker for Innovation. Haefele is highly knowledgeable and forward-thinking, yet still has a way of making complex topics completely accessible. If you're considering a website redesign for your library, this is a must-read resource.

—Ellyssa Kroski
Director of information technology

The New York Law Institute
http://www.ellyssakroski.com
http://ccgclibraries.com
ellyssakroski@yahoo.com

PREFACE

It's the twenty-first century—shouldn't your library's website reflect that? There's no need to manually maintain HTML code in dozens or hundreds of files anymore. WordPress lets you point and click your way to a useful and helpful website, with a user-friendly interface and plenty of help available.

WordPress makes it easy for any size staff or budget to keep your site modern and useful. Even if you have zero experience working on the web, WordPress is designed for you! This book will get you oriented and working productively.

Are you a web department of one? You can be up and running a WordPress site in less than ten minutes at zero cost. Are you part of a larger department with project hours and budget to spare? You can customize WordPress to your heart's content in simple yet powerful ways and pay only for the advanced features in your hosting. No matter your library's size or resources, this book will show you how to improve your website by building it in WordPress. With no previous knowledge, you'll learn how to set up a WordPress site from scratch and customize it to meet your patrons' needs. By the time you finish the last chapter you'll have the tools and knowledge to build your library a WordPress site and get many years of smooth operation out of it.

Chapters 1 through 3 will give you some background on how Word-Press works, walking you step-by-step through the basic setup and customization options. By the end of the third chapter you'll already have enough knowledge and guidance to create and run a simple WordPress site.

Chapter 4 shows you how libraries of all types have successfully put WordPress to work for their organizational websites. Examples and interviews from public, academic, school, and special librarians will give you great practical ideas for how you can design, build, and customize your own site.

Chapter 5 will provide you with step-by-step project instructions, walking you through how to build many of the features seen in those example library sites. You'll learn how to:

- use free plugins and themes to enhance your site
- build engaging image collections and online exhibits
- create your own child themes
- utilize powerful analytics programs to gather usage statistics
- utilize free tools for site-wide content analysis
- create your own shortcodes with automated content that can appear throughout your website
- and much more!

Chapter 6 discusses website security and disaster recovery as well as provides tips to keep your site secure, up to date, and easy to maintain.

Chapter 7 looks at the bright future of WordPress, and gives you an idea of what to expect as you build your expertise.

The Recommended Reading section is full of sources for digging deeper into whichever aspects of WordPress catch your eye.

Above all, the main message of this book is don't be intimidated by WordPress! As you'll see in this book, it's a powerful tool but also has a strong focus on being easy to use. No matter your level of experience, you can build a fully functional library WordPress site in less than a day. By the end of the book you'll know how to set up your site, how to customize the design, how to add the features your patrons want most, and how to do it all in a way that's simple to maintain.

Welcome to WordPress!

ACKNOWLEDGMENTS

This book would not have been possible without the assistance and knowledge of the colleagues who have taught me so much about Word-Press: Emily Brassell, Andy Jackson, Emily King, Steve Segedy, Tim Shearer, Kim Vassiliadis, and countless others. Thank you also to everyone who spoke with me about their library's use of WordPress. And to anyone who ever contributed to the WordPress Codex or other online documentation: a thousand appreciations. Extra thanks to Ellyssa Kroski, my editor, for her patience and guidance through the writing process.

Last and far from least, thank you, as always, to my wife and family for their eternal love and support.

1

AN INTRODUCTION TO WORDPRESS

WHAT IS WORDPRESS?

Library websites are living, breathing, and growing organisms. Without a system in place to manage your content, the sheer number of files can quickly overwhelm you and become impossible to manage. But WordPress is here to help! Without touching any code or doing any programming, you can set up a WordPress site totally customized to meet your exact needs. If you're an experienced coder, it's still all accessible for you to tinker with. But I can't emphasize enough that no programming is required. This book will walk you through setting things up step-by-step, helping you point and click your way to a modern and flexible library website.

Originally built as a blogging platform, WordPress later evolved into a content management system (CMS) capable of containing and organizing a website of virtually any size. Whether you need three pages or thousands (though I really hope you don't need thousands), WordPress offers a solution to fit your library's needs. Many of the tutorials for getting it set up and configured to meet those needs look intimidating, but it's easier than you might think. Even a coding novice can learn to make beautiful and functional WordPress websites in a matter of hours.

In this book you'll learn how to set up a WordPress site from scratch. You'll evaluate hosting options, understand the differences between versions of WordPress, work with plugins, and design your site's theme. After looking at examples of libraries using WordPress for inspiration, you'll tackle more advanced customizations and library related projects. Welcome aboard!

A LITTLE HISTORY

WordPress has been around since 2003, which makes it relatively ancient in web terms. But that age isn't a bad thing. Rather, it has allowed WordPress to grow and mature into a full-featured content management system.

Content management systems allow you to separate the content and presentation of your site from each other. When you need to add a page or update some text, you won't have to worry that your changes will break the layout of your site. WordPress will handle all navigation elements of your site, and give you tools to manage and edit each individual page. Your pages will all be searchable and can be easily optimized for search engines to find and index them. And because your content is stored separately from the layout of your site, it can be reformatted on the fly to match whatever device your visitors use to access your site. A WordPress site can look beautiful across any screen size: mobile, tablet, desktop, and beyond.

WORDPRESS AS OPEN SOURCE

For a long time WordPress excelled at the basics of blog display and management. Over the years it started adding more and more features, slowly turning into the great overall website CMS that it is today. It's not just for blogs anymore! How did that happen?

WordPress is an open source project, meaning anyone can download the raw source code and then either run it or modify it for free. This model is often referred to as "free as in kittens." Like kittens, you can get WordPress for free, but you will need to spend some time and resources to keep it clean and healthy.

Due to the open source nature of the project, WordPress has steadily improved and added features over the years. Today it stands as a shining example of what a modern web content management system can do. Like the best content management systems, you don't need to have a deep understanding of how the underlying technology works in order to produce and manage your content. Of course if you do understand how to use PHP (a common programming language) and MySQL (the type of database that WordPress uses) you can tweak WordPress to your heart's content, but that isn't required at all to use the software. Most of WordPress' functions have evolved to be accomplished entirely via point and click interfaces.

Today large sites like Time.com, sonymusic.com, and even Sweden's official website (Sweden.se) are all built on WordPress. As of October 2014, an estimated 23 percent of all sites on the web run WordPress to manage their content. Those sites saw a total of 4 billion page views in 2013! WordPress is a thriving, growing piece of software supported by a massive community of users and developers. You can take advantage of all their work and expertise, and build a website that's beautiful, functional, and (perhaps most importantly) maintainable. No experience required.

WORDPRESS IN LIBRARIES

With our often sprawling websites, libraries can usually benefit from content management tools. On the web, as in person, we need to be viewed as knowledgeable, friendly, and authoritative. Nothing hurts those perceptions more than a website that is out of date, inaccurate, or possibly even broken.

WordPress provides you with tools to manage your content, make it beautiful, and keep it current. Of course, there are countless other content management systems that can help you accomplish the same goals. Drupal and Joomla come to mind, and even LibGuides can be used as a general purpose website with some tweaking. But those tools can be hard to use. While they can help you build a wonderful website, WordPress has a swell of popularity behind it which makes it a superior candidate to run your site: a strong and active developer community ensures that bugs are fixed promptly and useful new features are added all the time. WordPress is easy to use now, and is only getting easier. With so many users behind it, they've produced a wealth of online documentation. If you run into a problem with WordPress, or want to add a feature to your site, odds are that a dozen people have had the exact same issue and worked through solutions already. And you can contribute too! Nothing feels better than giving back to the community.

This popularity also means that many of us in the library world already have experience using WordPress. Even if you've only used it to write a simple personal blog, you'll find that you already understand a surprising amount about how WordPress works. That gives you an instant leg up over learning any other content management system.

WordPress makes it easy to manage blocks of text on your website, using a feature called shortcodes. Do you have building usage or checkout policies that get displayed on multiple branch pages? Instead of updating each page individually, with shortcodes you can update the text in one place and have WordPress push it out across your site. See chapter 5 for more information about how this feature works.

But WordPress isn't just for managing text content. It has rich functions for managing and displaying multimedia, and can be used to display beautiful rotating collections of your images. See chapter 5 again for more information on how WordPress can be used to display images of your library or highlight one of your special collections.

Beyond text and images, WordPress can manage virtually any kind of content. It has a built-in link manager, for example, which can be used to manage the links to your online resources or recommended websites. If a link to one of your resources ever changes, you can update the link in just one place and be confident that it gets automatically updated across any page where it appears on your site. Chapter 3 goes into WordPress' link management tools in more detail.

Libraries need a content management strategy. After all, managing content is what we do! While WordPress can't create that strategy for you, it can help you carry it out in a sustainable way. If your website is in plain HTML files now, you're probably frustrated with just how difficult it can be to maintain those pages. If you work for a large organization, it isn't uncommon to have hundreds or even thousands of pages! That's too much for any one person or even a department to maintain, and you need to bring some focused tools to address this important problem. Chapter 5 describes one way to pull metadata about your pages for content analysis and update decisions.

No matter who or how many people work on your website, WordPress can handle it. It's easy to assign different levels of access to different users, and you can see who's working on each page at a glance. The page authors will use a writing interface that is remarkably similar to Microsoft Word and other word processing programs. Formatting text is as easy as highlighting and clicking a button.

As mentioned before, any content management system requires care and feeding to keep it updated and humming along safely and securely. WordPress is no exception. You'll need to check in on security concerns and keep your site updated with WordPress' latest versions. But it's easy! WordPress even does most of this maintenance work itself. Chapter 2 discusses some hosting options where you can outsource some security concerns to a third party. But even if you want or need to do it yourself, chapter 6 includes a discussion of important and simple security features and concerns in WordPress.

If you learn just one thing from this book, know that a good content management system will make your life much easier. Of course I hope that you find the book more useful than just that one fact, but it alone is still important. WordPress is just one option among many content management systems, but it is a flexible and mature option that would serve almost any library well.

2

GETTING STARTED

WHERE WILL YOUR WORDPRESS SITE LIVE?

Now that you've decided to build a WordPress site, many decisions need to be addressed. First off, where will your WordPress site live? A website of any kind, even simple plain HTML files outside of a content management system, requires a web server to serve them up to your users. WordPress requires a slightly more complex server environment, but one that is still fairly standard. In order to run a WordPress site you need a server which can accomplish two things: run PHP, and store data in a MySQL database. Your "Pages" and other content are stored in the MySQL database. Code written in the PHP scripting language retrieves that content from the database on demand, then formats it into the final webpage that your users see and interact with. If you don't have a compatible server available to you already, there are many third-party options to choose from. It's a standard enough server configuration that most hosts will have set it up for you already, and installing WordPress on it just takes the click of a button.

WordPress.com

WordPress is an open source project. The software's underlying code is freely available to anyone. Anybody can take it, modify it, and hopefully will contribute their changes back to the original project. As a side effect of this openness, it is possible to take the code and turn it into a for-pay commercial product. The free version of WordPress will always be available, but it is not the only version.

WordPress.com is one of these for-pay versions of WordPress. Founded in 2005, WordPress.com will host your site for you. As of May 2014, WordPress.com sites receive more than fourteen million collective hits per month.

WordPress.com will run the necessary servers for your site, and provide a number of other related services. One particular feature to note is that WordPress.com will take care of all security updates and fixes for you. See chapter 6 for more information on WordPress security and just how important it is.

While the site offers a free service tier, many libraries will probably want to run a site at one of their premium levels. The 3 GB of storage space allotted to the free tier is likely plenty for most library websites, but there are many limitations to the plan which libraries may find objectionable. For example, the free service limits you to a WordPress.com URL for your site. This address must be formatted along the lines of: yourlibrary.WordPress.com. Free WordPress.com sites also lack direct technical support options, and will display ads that you don't have control over. In addition, your options for customizing the display of your site are extremely limited.

Paid upgrades available at WordPress.com can be purchased a la carte or in bundles. The a la carte pricing quickly gets complicated, so I'll focus on the bundle options here.

- The "Premium" bundle at $99 per year will upgrade your site to 13 GB of storage space and will remove all ads. You will also be able to use your own domain name (which WordPress.com will register for you, included in this fee), e-mail WordPress.com directly for support, and enable advanced customization of your layout and display via CSS.
- The "Business" bundle is priced at $299 per year. It includes all of the features of "Premium," but also upgrades your storage to unlimited and adds live chat support. "Business" also makes a number of premium themes available for your site, which may ease development of your site's visual style and layout.
- WordPress.com also offers an "Enterprise" level of service, which adds analytics and even more customization options. However,

the $500 per month price tag may place it out of reach of many libraries.

Note that no matter which plan you choose on WordPress.com, your selection of WordPress plugins and theme options will be very limited. This means curtailed options for customization of the site, and many popular WordPress tips and tricks won't work at all.

WordPress.org

If you want to have full customization capability, the freedom to apply any theme or plugin, and the ability to use your library's non-WordPress domain all for free, the self-hosted WordPress.org version of Word-Press may be a viable option for you. For this option, your organization must find a server for the website. As mentioned before, it will need to run both PHP and MySQL. As of May 2015, your server must run PHP version 5.2.4 or greater and MySQL version 5.0 or greater. Most libraries opt for this self-hosted version of WordPress, often due to lower long-term costs and the full customization it offers. And even with this version of WordPress, installation still takes no more than a couple of clicks.

With WordPress.org you receive great power but must also shoulder great responsibility. Because the software is hosted on servers you control, you have full customization options. You can install any plugin you want, use any theme for your site's appearance, and modify any piece of WordPress' underlying code. But security and support become two tasks you must accomplish on an ongoing basis by yourself as well. You must always keep your WordPress version up to date to minimize security risks, but thankfully this is easy to do. More information on Word-Press security is in chapter 6. When it comes to support, a self-hosted installation of WordPress.org has no third party to call and help diagnose a bug or explain a feature. While this might sound limiting, remember that you have free access to the extensive documentation in the online WordPress Codex and your own local IT support and expertise.

While running your own security and support sound like daunting tasks (even if it's really not that bad), the flexibility afforded by using a self-hosted WordPress installation is a significant gain over using the

WordPress.com service. Most later chapters in this book will assume or require that your site is running a self-hosted WordPress.org installation, but any features and projects which will also work on a WordPress.com account will be noted.

HOSTING OPTIONS FOR SELF-RUN WORDPRESS

If you'd like to build your site on the WordPress.org version of the platform but don't have the staffing expertise or hardware to run your own web server, other easy options are available. While you can download the WordPress software for free, you still need a service provider to host and run it for you. Your in-house IT department might fit that bill, or for a fee you can have a third-party company host your copy of the software. While these services are not free, they are almost always cheaper than paying for a premium WordPress.com plan.

ONE-CLICK INSTALLATION

Many web hosting companies offer to handle installation of many pieces of software, including WordPress, for you. While the phrase "One-Click Installation" may be a bit inaccurate, it's still not a huge exaggeration. These hosting providers will get a WordPress site up and running for you within a few minutes with minimal effort on your part. You won't need to manually create a database, upload the WordPress source files, or do any of the usual initial WordPress configuration

Table 2.1.   Comparison between Versions of WordPress

	WordPress.org	WordPress.com
Customization Options	Extensive	Limited
Price	Free, plus hosting fees of about $10 per month	Ranges from free to $500 per month
Your Server Requirements	MySQL and PHP	None
Plugins Available	Thousands	About twenty
Support Available	Extensive documentation and forums are available online	Customer support available with paid upgrade

steps. It is important to note that you will still be responsible for security and maintenance of your site when using this kind of hosting service. Your hosting company will usually not provide answers to your questions about WordPress or issues you encounter beyond the initial setup. But the barrier to entry for getting your site up and running is significantly lowered. I recommend picking a hosting company that has been around for years with a reputation for responsive customer service. Here are a few that fit the bill.

Dreamhost (www.Dreamhost.com)

Dreamhost is an excellent general purpose option for hosting any website, including one built on WordPress. Their pricing starts at about $8.95 per month, and Dreamhost offers the simplest possible WordPress installation process on this type of server. Your site can be active in as little as five minutes after creating an account.

Bluehost (www.Bluehost.com)

Much like Dreamhost, Bluehost is a general purpose web hosting option that happens to support WordPress well. Their plans usually start at about $5.99 per month, but Bluehost also occasionally offers sales as low as $2.95 per month for your first year.

WP Engine (www.WPengine.com)

For a more full service option, you may wish to host your site with WPengine.com. With plans starting at $29 per month, WP Engine will host your WordPress website and do much of the installation and maintenance for you. This is the full WordPress.org version of the software, meaning you will keep access to full customization options. WP Engine also provides some interesting and useful features on top of what you'd get out of the box from one-click install providers or hosting your own server: If you're familiar with using Git to manage your code, you can use it for development on your WP Engine site. They provide a staging area for new designs and features that you might add to your site, enabling you to test them before deploying the updates to your public site. WP Engine also offers robust backup and restore options for your site, and promise to do everything they can to block attacks against your site. And in the rare event a site does get hacked, they promise to fix it.

INTRODUCTION TO WORDPRESS THEMES

One of the most important decisions in building your WordPress site is choosing your theme. A WordPress theme controls the layout and design of your site. With a few clicks a theme can make your site look like a newspaper, blog, e-commerce site, or pretty much any kind of website you can think of. While you could build a theme from scratch, it is often useful (and definitely easier) to start with a theme someone else already developed. Using the self-hosted version of WordPress, you will be able to tweak and build upon what someone else has already accomplished. Some themes are free and others have a fee or subscription associated with them, but plan on spending some fun time trying out different themes early in your design process.

Browsing Themes

Picking a theme is a fun part of the WordPress process. There's some amazing designers out there working with themes, and it's easy to lose hours being blown away by what's possible. WordPress.org/themes is home to over 2,500 free themes. You can filter that huge list by using options like dominant color, number of columns in the design, and many more criteria. Themeforest.net is another giant repository of WordPress themes, with over 4,000 for sale. Themeforest's themes aren't free, but are generally very reasonably priced. As I write this, the most expensive theme on the site is $60, and many are much less. All of these themes show off amazing designs, and we get to take advantage of all this completed work!

Working with a Theme

WordPress themes are simply collections of files that tell WordPress how to display your content. You can access your site's theme options via the WordPress administration menus. After logging in, hold your mouse over "Appearance" in the black menu on the left side of your page, then click "Themes." Any themes you've installed on your site will be listed here. If you're using WordPress.com, you'll see their list of pre-installed themes. Clicking the "Activate" button on a theme will turn it on for your site. After that one click, every visitor to your site will see the new theme in action. So make sure it's what you want before activation!

The "Live Preview" feature is especially useful when experimenting with different themes. Hold your mouse over the theme you'd like to preview, and click the "Live Preview" button that appears. A new page will open, showing you what your site would look like if you choose to activate the theme. You can even do some basic customizations of colors and layout options in the menu on the left side of your screen. Note that exactly which customization options you see will vary depending on the theme you've chosen. When it's all set to your liking, you can click "Save & Activate" near the upper left corner to switch on the theme for the world to see.

If you change your mind about a color or other customization choice later, you can always go back to the "Appearance" section of WordPress' administration menus and change it. The "Customize and Theme Options" sections are available there. More advanced theme customization is covered in chapter 5.

Adding a New Theme

The WordPress Theme Directory is a massive repository of potential themes. More than 2,500 of them are currently available. Along with featured themes on the directory's homepage, you can also search and filter potential themes by criteria like color, layout, and specific features. Responsive layout themes in particular may be good choices, as they can ensure that your site displays well on desktops, tablets, and mobile phones without any extra design work or maintenance on your part.

To search new themes, click "Appearance" in WordPress' administration menus. Next, click the "Add New Theme" option in the main body of the page. Now you'll see a selection of featured and popular themes, as well as the ability to filter the options you want by clicking "Feature Filter" near the top of the page.

Clicking on any theme will show you a preview of what the theme looks like. If you like it, click the blue "Install" button near the upper left corner. WordPress will add the theme to your site. Now you can preview your content in the theme and activate it as described earlier in this section.

Not all themes are listed in the official WordPress directory. If you purchase or download a theme from another vendor, installing it follows a slightly different process. These themes will download as a .zip file. To add it to your site, go back to the "Themes" section of your "Appearance" menu. Near the top of the page click on "Add New." On the next screen, again at the top, click "Upload Theme" to upload the .zip file you saved above. Now the theme will appear in your Themes administration menu just like any other theme, and can be previewed or activated the same way.

Advanced theme customization and maintenance is covered in chapter 5.

Now that we've covered installation options and themes, let's talk about the main features and functionality that you'll find in WordPress.

3

TOOLS AND APPLICATIONS

MAIN FEATURES AND FUNCTIONALITY

WordPress has developed into a very user-friendly tool. Most tasks can be accomplished in a point and click–type environment, with very little manual customization of code. While WordPress lists things like "simplicity" and "flexibility" among its major features (and they're certainly true), those words don't necessarily tell you what it can do or how it works in practice. This chapter provides a more practical tour of the interface and available features. We'll specifically look at the self-hosted version of WordPress (see chapter 2 for more about what this means), as it has the most available features and flexibility.

After installing your WordPress site (covered in depth in the previous chapter), your site will at first have a number of default settings and options applied to it. Your site will look much like this one, which I've aptly named Demo Site (see figure 3.1).

Don't worry, we'll do some easy design work soon. Your final site won't look anything like a blog.

Note that this default site is designed to be responsive. This means that the site will reformat itself to display nicely on screens of any width. Whether your users arrive on a desktop computer, tablet, phone, or something else yet to be invented, they will be presented with a readable experience that requires minimal scrolling and zooming to view your content. Not all WordPress sites are responsive, but recent devel-

Figure 3.1.   An uncustomized WordPress site.

opments in WordPress themes and plugins (see chapters 2 and 5) make it easy to keep your site flexible.

Also note the navigation on the left hand side of the site. This is automatically generated by WordPress, and requires no coding at all on your part. The "Recent Posts" section will always display your latest content, and "Recent Comments" will do the same for any comments. Links to navigate to past posts by month are automatically put under "Archives," and any categories you assign to your posts will do the same in the "Categories" section. Users can also search all of your site with the box in the upper left corner. The tagline "Just Another WordPress Site" above the search box can be changed or removed in the administrative options.

WordPress has also provided a small bit of content in a sample post ("Hello World!"), just so your site isn't entirely empty.

LOGGING IN

To log in to your WordPress site, look near the bottom left corner. In the "Meta" section of links, one of them says "Log in." Click that to get to the standard WordPress Username and Password prompts. But before you log in, bookmark this page (it will always be http://yoursiteaddress.org/wp-admin/). Depending on how you customize your site going forward, that link may not always be visible in that corner of your site. You'll want to be able to find your way back to it.

DASHBOARD

After logging in, you're greeted by WordPress' Dashboard. This page is designed to give you an overview of the status of your site. Recent posts, pages, and comments are all displayed along with updates from Word-Press about the software itself and a box to jot down a quick draft of new content. Most of WordPress' administrative options are listed in two black bars visible on this page. The black bar at the top of your screen provides some shortcuts for creating content. But more importantly, that black bar is where you'll log out. Hold your mouse over your username in the upper right corner of your screen to display the log out option. This top bar will always appear while you're logged in, even when you're viewing your finished WordPress site as if you were a regular site visitor. This provides easy administrative commands accessible as you browse around the site. Now, look at the second black menu bar. This one is on the left side of your screen (see figure 3.2).

If you don't see the black sidebar, your browser may be too narrow. Maximize it to restore the links. These links are the main sections for creating and maintaining your site. We'll look at them one by one, but remember you can always get back to the Dashboard by clicking the "Dashboard" link at the top of the menu.

POSTS

The "Posts" section is where you'll perhaps obviously manage any posts on your site. WordPress has two main content types: *Posts* and *Pages*. WordPress defines *Posts* as "entries listed in reverse chronological order." Think of *Posts* as a traditional blog homepage, with the most recent post displayed at the top and older ones visible as you scroll down the page. *Pages*, on the other hand, are for longer term content, which doesn't need to be displayed in any kind of chronological order. Your library hours should be contained on a *Page*, for example, since that's pretty static and permanent content. *Posts* should be used for

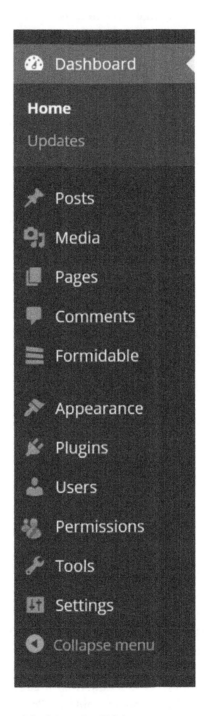

Figure 3.2.   WordPress Administrative Sidebar

more of a blog style of content. Again, if your content is less ephemeral, such as a list of library policies or links to electronic resources, it should be created as a *Page* instead (see below). Use *Posts* for content like announcements of library events, temporary e-resource outages, or any other purpose you may already use a blog for.

In the main section of the page you'll see the "Hello World!" default *Post* that WordPress created for you. Hold your mouse over that "Hello World!" text to reveal some management options for the *Post*. From there you can Edit, Trash (delete), or View it. Note that clicking "View" will take you back to the public view of that *Post* on your site. Click that "Edit" option to move to the "Edit Post" screen.

By default, you will be viewing your *Post* in text mode. Text mode is essentially writing in HTML. You'll need to do the formatting with code yourself, though there are a few shortcut buttons at the top of the editor to help out. If you'd prefer to write and format in a style more like Microsoft Word, click on the "Visual" tab above the main edit box for your *Post*. Now you can highlight text and use the commands at the top of the edit box (bold, italics, bullet points, etc.) to format your content.

You can also change the title of your *Post* at the top of the screen. Other options on this page include assigning Categories and Tags to your *Post*, which influence how users can find your content. The options in the "Publish" box in the upper right corner are particularly important to notice. This is where you can change the Status and Visibility of your *Post*, which controls who can see your content.

Directly above the edit box, there is an "Add Media" button. This is used to insert images, audio, or video into your *Post*. More on working with media is in the next section of this chapter.

Once you've made any changes, click the blue "Update" button on the right side of the screen to save your content.

To start a new *Post* from scratch, click on *Posts* again in the left side black bar. Now click "Add New" in one of two locations: the left side black bar, or the button above your list of *Posts*. Note that with a new *Post* you have the option to save it as a draft instead of immediately publishing it for public view. A saved draft will appear in the *Posts* list with a note that it is only a draft. You can also use the "Preview" button to see what your content will look like without actually publishing it yet.

MEDIA: ADDING IMAGES AND VIDEO

The media section of the black menu bar (see figure 3.2) is the media library where you will manage any images, audio, or video used on your site. Like with *Posts*, there's an "Add New" button. Click it to bring up an upload screen. Note that by default the maximum upload size for a media item is 7 MB. While it is possible to work around this limit, for video in particular you will probably get better results by uploading your file to a site like YouTube instead and then embedding the video on your WordPress site.

After you've uploaded a sample item, click "Media" in the black menu bar again to go back to your main media library. You should now see your uploaded file or files listed. Hold your mouse over any one item to see some management options including Edit and Delete. For now, click on "Edit."

The "Edit" screen for media allows you to add a caption, alternative text (this will appear in your image's HTML alt tag, which is great for accessibility), and a description. Filling out as much of this information as you can seems like a drag at the time, but will make it much easier to manage and use your media later. At the very least, give your image a descriptive title at the top of the screen.

Immediately below the image itself on the Edit screen is an "Edit Image" button. This brings up some basic image editing options such as cropping and rotating.

Now that you've added an image, you can use it when editing a *Post* or *Page*. While editing your text content, click the "Add Media" button. Here you can search through your media library to find the image you want. Click the thumbnail to select it, and then make sure to set the alignment and size display options in the lower right corner before you click "Insert Into Page." WordPress automatically generates different size versions of your image, which is useful for making sure you don't waste users' (or your own) bandwidth with an image that's larger than it needs to be.

PAGES

Pages may appear similar to *Posts* at first glance, but understanding how they differ from *Posts* is crucial to organizing and maintaining your WordPress site. WordPress defines *Pages* as "static and not listed by date." While *Posts* are displayed in reverse chronological order like a blog, *Pages* are much more standalone. For example, you should use *Pages* for content like a Library Policies page or a list of your electronic resources. This content is relatively permanent and fits into the main navigation of your site. *Pages* often appear in your WordPress main menu by default, while *Posts* will not.

Working with *Pages* is very similar to working with *Posts*. Holding your mouse over a *Page* in the list brings up management options, including Edit. Clicking "Edit" takes you to the same Edit screen that you saw for a *Post*. Once again, you can write in either Visual or Text mode and save a new *Page* as a draft if you aren't finished with it yet.

COMMENTS

The "Comments" section of the black menu bar is where you go to manage any comments left by users on your site. Both *Posts* and *Pages* can have comments. While many WordPress sites choose to disable comments entirely to ease the burden of managing both legitimate and spam comments, you do have some powerful administrative options here. You can approve comments, delete them, and reply to them. Once again, hold your mouse over a comment to view the administrative options.

If you want to disable comments on your site entirely, look a little further down the black menu sidebar (see figure 3.2). Click on "Settings" there, and a sub-menu will appear. Click "Discussion" in that sub-menu. Now look for the option labeled "Allow people to post comments on new articles" and uncheck the box next to it. Lastly, scroll all the way to the bottom of the page, and click the blue "Save Changes" button to remove comments from your site. Comments can also be enabled or disabled for each individual *Page* of your site while editing each *Page* or *Post*.

APPEARANCE

The "Appearance" section of the black menu bar is the first one to contain many sub-menus and customization options. After clicking "Appearance," you'll see sub-menus in the black bar for Themes, Customize, Widgets, Menus, Header, Background, and Editor.

Themes

A theme is a preset list of display options you can apply to your site. It's made up of some combination of color schemes, custom layouts, advanced menu options, background images, and pretty much any other design element you can think of. This is a pretty important topic, so we'll come back to it later. For information on working with themes (including the "Customize" menu item here), see chapter 5.

Widgets

Widgets give you an easy way to add reusable boxes of content to certain areas of your site. A widget might be a block of text, search bar, or menu for your site. You can easily add these widgets to your footer or sidebar. The Widgets sub-menu controls the small blocks of content you see in those parts of your public site. By dragging and dropping items to or from the Primary Sidebar and other sections on the right side of the page, you can control things like whether your site has a search box or whether your sidebar links to recent comments on your site. Clicking on an individual widget's title will also often reveal more options relevant to that content. The Text widget is particularly useful, allowing you to put blocks of custom text in your sidebar or footer. Exactly which regions you can add a widget to will vary depending on your theme, but the default theme includes a Primary Sidebar, Content Sidebar, and Footer Widget Area.

Menus

Any WordPress site with more than a few *Pages* will need a menu, and this is where you go to create it. Note that out of the box, your site has no menu at all. Give your new menu a name on this page. Something straightforward like "main menu" is often useful. Then click the blue "Create Menu" button on the right side.

Now, on the left side of this page you can see a list of your *Pages*. If you want a *Page* to appear in your menu, check the box next to it and click "Add to Menu." You also have options here to add a link to an external site (something like Google Scholar, for example) or a link to all your *Pages* labeled with a given Category to your menu. After you've added all of the items that you want in your menu, you can drag and drop your menu items to reorder them. To create a drop-down menu, drag one menu item on top of another one.

In order to make your menu actually display on your website, you'll need to check a box in the "Theme Locations" setting on this page. In the default theme, you can check a box to have your menu appear at either the top or left side of your *Pages*. Exactly which menu locations are available to you will vary depending on the theme you've chosen. Almost all themes contain at least two, the top horizontal menu and a vertical menu on the left side of the *Page*. You can create different menus for each location. For libraries, this is a useful way to separate out your types of content. The top horizontal menu is a great place to list the major sections of your site like the catalog, hours, a blog, or branch locations. This menu gets the most visual attention, so put the major items there. By reserving this menu for relatively few items, you make it easier for patrons to notice and use it at a glance. The vertical menu can be used to help patrons stay oriented to where they are in your site, with a more complete and detailed listing of the *Pages* available to them.

Note that *Posts* cannot be added to a menu. Only *Pages* are eligible to display there.

Depending on your site's theme and plugins, you may have multiple menus to pick from. For example, you may have a main dropdown style navigation and also a quick links menu on the left or right side of the page. This varies by theme. For more on themes, see chapters 2 and 5.

Header

The "Header" section of the "Appearance" menu is where you can upload an image to appear in the header of your site. You also have options to hide text on your header or change the color of that text.

Because the exact size of your header will change based on the theme you choose for your site, hold off on setting this up for now. Come back and pick an image once you have a theme in place.

Background

Setting a background image for your site is not supported by all themes. If you upload a background image here and don't see it on your site, check whether your theme supports backgrounds. The default Word-Press theme does not support backgrounds.

Editor

The "Editor" section of the "Appearance" menu is for advanced cus-tomization. This is where you can edit the CSS and PHP files used in your theme. Unless you are already familiar with CSS and PHP, you can pretend the "Editor" section doesn't exist. While you can make all kinds of changes to your site here, it's often much easier to do it in the other option menus mentioned above. As a side note, editing your theme in this way will also make it very difficult to apply any update released for your theme. For more on this problem, and how to avoid it, see chapter 5.

PLUGINS

WordPress has thousands of plugins available. Often developed by third-party programmers, a plugin will provide some enhanced func-tionality or options for your site. Many of the projects in chapter 5 involve using plugins.

Introduction to WordPress Plugins

A WordPress plugin provides additional functionality to your site that isn't supported by WordPress by default. A plugin might add an event calendar or allow you to accept donations via credit card. Often created by individuals who wanted to see an extra feature on their site, Word-

Press notes that a plugin can "do almost anything you can imagine." In my experience that's entirely correct! A plugin might watch your site's comments for spam, create more complex menu navigation, allow you to easily create forms for your site, provide enhanced security options, let you create simple and beautiful image galleries, or limit your administrative users' access to various functions. The list of features plugins can add is almost endless. And like themes, many of the most popular and useful WordPress plugins are available for free.

Why Use a Plugin?

Plugins let you customize your WordPress site to do just about anything you want. If you wish WordPress did something differently, there's probably a plugin created that does exactly that. Because WordPress is an open source project, anyone can write their own plugin to modify how the system works. Many people have done this, and they often choose to make this code available for others in the form of a plugin. You should definitely take advantage of all that hard work!

Working With a Plugin

To view your list of installed plugins, click the "Plugins" menu option on the left side of your WordPress administrator screen (see figure 3.1). Now you'll see a list of installed plugins, although if this is the first time you've looked here it will be a mostly blank list. By default, every Word-Press website comes with a plugin called "Hello Dolly." If enabled, the plugin will display a lyric from the song "Hello, Dolly" on every page of your administrative interface. If that isn't a feature you want, feel free to click on the red "Delete" link to remove it. This plugin is included mainly to provide an example of how plugins work.

Adding a plugin is a simple two-step process. First you install it, and then you activate it. If you install a plugin but don't activate it, it won't do anything. To install a plugin, click "Plugins" in your administrator menu again. In the list that appears below "Plugins," click "Add New." You can now search and filter through all plugins listed in the official WordPress Plugin Directory. There's over thirty thousand of them!

After finding the plugin you want, click "Install Now." After the installation finishes (it'll just take a few seconds), click "Activate Plugin."

The plugin will now appear in the "Plugins" list of your administrative interface. If a plugin has settings, you can access them from that list.

Not all plugins are included in the official directory. It's not unusual to purchase one from a third party. Luckily, installing them still isn't difficult. On the "Add New" page for plugins that you visited above, look for the link that says "upload a plugin in .zip format via this page." When you bought your plugin, you should have received a .zip file from the seller. This is where you can upload that .zip to add the plugin to your page. Don't forget to activate it afterward.

If you see unexpected behavior or display issues on your site, it's possible that a plugin may be having unintended consequences. An easy way to troubleshoot this is to return to your plugins list and deactivate them one by one. Check your site after each deactivation to see if the issue is resolved. With a little trial and error, you can track down which plugin is the culprit. A deactivated plugin retains all of its settings and can be reactivated from the same menu with one click.

The creator of a plugin may choose to release an update which adds new features or fixes bugs. WordPress will alert you when an update to one of your plugins is available and will walk you through the updating process.

More information on working with plugins, along with specific and recommended examples, is in chapter 5. But feel free to play with them now! Plugins are just as easy to remove as they are to add, so there's no harm in getting used to how they work and seeing how they can enhance your site.

USERS

If more than one library staff member will be working on your website, the "Users" section of the black menu bar is very important. This is where you can create or delete users, and also change their role on the site. Different roles have different levels of access:

- *Administrators* can access all options and make changes to anything on the site.
- An *Editor* can publish and manage all *Posts* and *Pages*.
- Each *Author* can only manage the *Pages* and *Posts* they created.

- *Contributors* can write drafts, but can't publish them to the public site.
- *Subscribers* can only manage their own profile information. This category of user is not useful for the vast majority of library websites.

TOOLS

The "Tools" menu allows you to export your content or import it from another WordPress site. While other more robust backup options exist, this is a simple way to back up your *Posts*, *Pages*, menus, and other content.

SETTINGS

The "Settings" menu is quite extensive and could likely stand having a chapter or entire book to itself. But the best way to figure out all the settings available is to simply browse through them. Most are self-explanatory, and broken down into sections: General, Writing, Reading, Discussion, Media, and Permalinks. These are a few of the more important settings to be aware of:

Timezone

Located in the General settings menu, the "Timezone" option affects how any timestamps on your content displays on your site. If you don't set it to your local zone, the times will display incorrectly.

Front Page Displays

The setting labeled "Front Page Displays" in the "Reading" section of the settings is crucial to how users first encounter your website. By default this is set to "Your latest posts." If left alone, this means that your WordPress homepage will function like a blog and only show your latest *Posts* in reverse chronological order. If you want your WordPress site to function like a blog, then you can leave this alone. But if you want more control over your homepage or don't want it to look like a blog at all, this is where you can change it up. Step back earlier in this chapter and create a *Page* that you want to use as your homepage. Then come back to this "Front Page Displays" setting and set it to "A static page." You'll be asked to pick a *Page* to use as your homepage, so just select the one you've created for this purpose. If you don't have a *Page* created to use as your homepage yet, go back to the *Pages* section of the black menu bar (see earlier in this chapter and figure 3.2) to create one before changing this setting.

Permalinks

By default, the *Posts* and *Pages* you create in WordPress don't have very human readable URLs. A *Post* might be mylibrary.net/?p=123, for example, and links to *Pages* often look like mylibrary.net/?page_id=2. The "Permalink" settings let you change that format to something a bit more friendly.

- If your WordPress site is primarily a blog, a setting that puts the date in the URL like the "Day and name" option here might be desireable. This way your *Post* URLs will look like: mylibrary.net/2015/03/04/postTitle.
- If your site will primarily function as a non-blog traditional website, you might pick the "Post name" option. This creates URLs for your *Posts* and *Pages* more like mylibrary.net/postTitle and mylibrary.net/pageTitle.

No matter what permalink format you pick, choose it early in your development process and stick with it. Changing a permalink structure after a site has launched means that all of your URLs will change. Any bookmarks that users have saved will break, and all the links to your site in search engines will no longer work either.

WRAP-UP

By now you've gotten a bit of a feel for how WordPress works. You know how to configure your site enough to do some basic customizations, and you've also seen how WordPress manages *Posts* and *Pages*. But how does a WordPress site get set up in the first place? How can you find a test site to play with? The next two chapters will walk you through this important part of the process.

4

LIBRARY EXAMPLES AND CASE STUDIES

There are so many libraries of all kinds making good use of WordPress. While it can be useful to browse around the web and look at any website that uses WordPress, that would be a ton of sites to look at.

Narrowing your examples to WordPress sites created by and for libraries will give you a better sample. They've probably solved many of the same challenges and met the same goals that you face in your own work. We're a sharing profession, and that extends far into the web world. Looking at other libraries' websites as case studies is an excellent way to familiarize yourself with what WordPress can do early in your project.

The "Libraries Using WordPress" page of the lib20 wiki (http://lib20. pbworks.com/w/page/59677899/WordPress-Libraries-examples) has a huge list of WordPress-friendly libraries for you to browse. This chapter will take an in-depth look at many examples. For each of these case studies, someone involved with the creation of the WordPress site generously agreed to answer my questions for this book. We can all learn from their experiences and wonderful results. We'll look at libraries in four categories:

- academic libraries
- public libraries
- K–12 libraries and media centers
- special libraries

ACADEMIC LIBRARY EXAMPLES

University of Wisconsin-Madison General Library System

Dave Luke, technology services coordinator, and Jessie Nemec, information processing consultant at UW-Madison
Website: https://www.library.wisc.edu/

The University of Wisconsin-Madison General Library System's website is a great example of what a responsive WordPress site can look like (see figure 4.1). No matter what kind of device you use to access the site, it formats itself well for your screen.

They built their own theme from the ground up, which let them completely customize the site for their local users' needs. In addition to the general public, their library serves 43,000 students and an additional 22,000 faculty and staff. WordPress works well even at this scale, much larger than many libraries face.

I particularly like the menu design on this site. WordPress' flexibility shows through in the way that each top-level menu item expands out into a larger pane with options and explanations about the links available. This navigation is automatically consistent throughout the site,

Figure 4.1.   University of Wisconsin-Madison Library Homepage

giving users a consistent experience and way to navigate around the pages.

UW-Madison has taken advantage of many common plugins to enhance their site. They use Gravity Forms to create and manage their contact forms. Advanced Custom Fields lets them tweak and customize their *Page* and *Post* edit screens, and Migrate DB Pro assists with moving WordPress between servers.

There are also some subtle animations incorporated into the design, such as the way the search box expands out when you visit the homepage. Too much animation can get in the way of users accomplishing their tasks on your website, but applied smartly like this it can help to make your WordPress site look modern and inviting. This kind of animation is often included in a theme, so you might want to keep it in mind when selecting yours.

Dave Luke, technology services coordinator, and Jessie Nemec, information processing consultant at UW-Madison generously answered some of my questions about how they use WordPress to run their website.

They started using WordPress very recently in 2014. They're happy enough with it that UW-Madison will be expanding their WordPress installation to include more of their domains in the near future.

Like many academic libraries using WordPress, Luke and Nemec noted that they found significant support for using WordPress on campus. It's very possible that your university website is already on WordPress! Your central campus IT organization may even have site licenses for some paid plugins or themes that you can take advantage of.

UW-Madison's site is also a great example of a large organization using WordPress with support from many different staff members. They have dozens of content editors, one designer, one server and database technician, plus some general technical support staff available. None of these staff need to be 100 percent devoted to WordPress though—they spend at most 25 percent of their time working on the website.

I asked Luke and Nemec how well they thought WordPress meets the needs of their users. They made an excellent point: "With good design and technical support, the user should have no idea what kind of backend we are using." While I love WordPress and think it's a great solution for library websites, users won't necessarily be so excited about the technical details. But that's the great thing about WordPress—as we see with UW-Madison's site, it can provide an amazing, completely transparent experience to library users.

University of North Carolina at Chapel Hill Libraries

Kim Vassiliadis, head of user experience
Website: http://library.unc.edu

UNC Chapel Hill University Libraries went live with their main website in WordPress in August 2013. I work at UNC Chapel Hill and was heavily involved in this project. Kim Vassiliadis is Head of User Experience at UNC Chapel Hill Libraries, and spoke with me about the details of the process.

UNC's library website, like many seen in these case studies, is responsive (see figure 4.2). Serving about 30,000 students and 4,000 faculty, it needed to be able to work on any device they might choose to

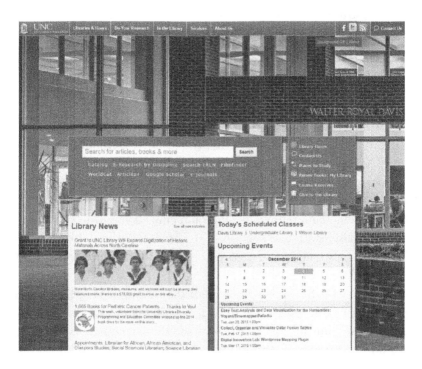

Figure 4.2.   University of North Carolina at Chapel Hill Library Homepage

access the website on. Their site runs on a heavily customized version of the "Responsive" theme (Note that "Responsive" is both the actual name of theme and also a descriptor here). UNC's site designers specifically wanted to emphasize the physical spaces of the campus libraries, so the homepage prominently features a rotating photo of library facilities. This element carries over into the background of all other pages too and is a great showcase for how WordPress can highlight and show off images.

Again, like many libraries moving to WordPress, this was UNC's libraries' first true content management system. Previous development on the website was done directly using templates in HTML, PHP, and CSS.

Despite differences in scale between different academic libraries, many of their steps are universal. UNC Chapel Hill took about six months of development in WordPress to get the site up and running, a timeline that can probably be adopted by libraries of any size. And no matter the size of your library or institution, at some point you'll probably need to train someone on how to use WordPress to make updates to your site. Vassiliadis noted that this is her favorite thing about WordPress: it takes her about ten minutes to train someone to make page updates, compared to the hour or more it took on the pre-WordPress site.

Like UW-Madison, UNC Chapel Hill has several content editors responsible for keeping pieces of the site current and updated. The User Experience team provides guidance and works with a team of developers to maintain and enhance features on the site.

Also like most WordPress sites, UNC Chapel Hill libraries makes extensive use of plugins to customize the look and function of their pages. These are some of their favorite recommended plugins:

- Press Permit handles customizing access rules for different accounts.
- Elegant Themes allows for easy layout design and access to common visual elements via simple shortcodes (see chapter 5 for more about shortcodes).
- Formidable has simple but powerful controls for designing and managing forms on a site.

- Broken Link Checker quickly e-mails staff when any *Page* or *Post* contains a broken link.
- Media Library Assistant is useful for tagging and organizing multimedia content like images.

Vassiliadis also noted that WordPress didn't fit all of UNC's content. It can be a daunting task to think about uniting all the different sources of content an academic library uses under one umbrella. Early in the development process, UNC decided to use WordPress for the main library website but still allow some content to live elsewhere.

The catalog, for example, can't be realistically put into WordPress. But by editing the headers in the catalog, UNC was able to move some of the visual elements of their WordPress theme into these other systems. They now share the same layout for a dropdown menu, for example. Their Libguides and other systems were similarly edited. Little bits of extra work like this can go a long way toward providing that seamless experience for visitors that all library websites strive for. Like UW-Madison, UNC Chapel Hill didn't want the user to have to care or even know what system they were using. Thanks to WordPress' flexibility, this goal was easy to accomplish.

PUBLIC LIBRARY EXAMPLES

Radnor Memorial Library

Molly Carroll Newton, coordinator of community relations and
    young adult programming
Website: http://www.radnorlibrary.org

Located in Wayne, Pennsylvania, Radnor Public Library serves around 15,000 residents, with half between the ages of forty and seventy-four. Their township contains four college campuses and most residents are tech-savvy. The local high school even provides iPads for all students!

Radnor Public Library has been using WordPress since the beginning of 2012, which makes them a pretty early adopter of WordPress in the library world. Like so many library websites, their previous website was maintained in plain HTML. The current WordPress site was de-

Figure 4.3.   Radnor Memorial Library Homepage

signed by an outside company, and Molly Carroll Newton spoke to me about how she manages their content.

The Radnor Public Library website is an excellent reminder that WordPress started life primarily as a blogging system (see figure 4.3). It has since evolved to be the capable whole website management system you've mastered in this book, but it still does blogging well too. Radnor's adult program coordinator and children's librarian each have blogs contained within the broader umbrella of their WordPress site. And I'm especially impressed that they've done all this design and content organization without using any WordPress plugins at all. Radnor Library's website is an excellent example of just how powerful WordPress can be right out of the box—without tons of tweaking under the hood. Their layout is simple, clean, modern, and easy to read and navigate. Their chosen theme was customized, but in a way that requires minimal maintenance as updates are made. Newton is the only person managing the Radnor Library website, other than a few who have access in an emergency. She only needs to spend a few hours a week updating and maintaining the library's site, and it's all done in-house.

Radnor is a great example of how a small library can use WordPress to rein in their web presence and make it more maintainable by the staff already on hand at the library. You don't need to have a huge team of developers to get an attractive and maintainable site set up in Word-

Press. With a little bit of work at the start, a single person can often maintain the site going forward.

Radnor's customized header provides a great introduction to the library, tying their virtual presence and physical location together by showing off images of their staff, visitors, and spaces. The library's contact information and hours are both prominently displayed in the header of every page, immediately answering two of the most common reasons someone visits a library website.

These are also great examples of how WordPress can be used to make creating and updating website content easier. By storing their hours in the header just once, any changes to the hours just have to be made in that one place. In a plain HTML system, hours would have to be hand-edited on each individual page. Not only does the WordPress method save staff time, but it also makes it much harder to miss updating a page.

Like many of the libraries I spoke to for this book, Newton noted how easy it is to train other staff to use WordPress. She finds WordPress "extremely user-friendly, and [it] allows us to do a lot of different things without HTML." Ease of use was also one of the big plusses that drew them to WordPress in the first place. Radnor Library's website is hosted by a third party, Network Solutions.

Feedback from their patrons has been extremely positive, and Newton also likes that they can be informed of library activities immediately from the library's homepage. Newton has plans to add more pages to the site in the future, and feels very comfortable doing this work herself.

Jackson District Library

Michael Greenlee, digital services specialist
Website: http://www.myjdl.com

Jackson District Library (JDL) in Jackson County, Michigan, serves a population of around 160,000. Michael Greenlee, digital services specialist, describes many areas of their district as quite rural and notes that securing high-speed Internet access is a challenge for some. One of JDL's goals is to encourage tech-savviness among their patrons and give them access to the means of creation with technology.

Figure 4.4.   Jackson District Library Homepage

Greenlee was hired in September 2013, and immediately began work on redesigning the library's website (see figure 4.4). Previously hosted in Drupal, the library was looking to go another direction and liked the themes and templates they saw available for WordPress. They chose a theme called Churchope, available for $48 at http://churchope. themoholics.com/.

JDL's launch of their WordPress site came about six months after Greenlee started work. Like many WordPress users, JDL relies on a number of plugins for site design and maintenance. Greenlee highlighted a few:

- User Role Editor manages user roles and capabilities.
- Clean Up Images deletes all unused images not referred to by any *Post* or *Page*.
- Search & Replace is useful for replacing text directly in your WordPress database. Greenlee notes, "This was really helpful for us because we developed the site on a virtual machine localhost. Before going live we needed to change a lot of URLs."
- Akismet, which Greenlee calls "the standard bearer for WordPress spam protection."

JDL took a very user-centered approach to the design of their site in WordPress. Greenlee describes some of their thought process:

> The vast majority of users who visit our WordPress site will immediately do a search in the catalog widget and cross over into the catalog interface. Visitors to the site are definitely task-orientated and two tasks they are the most interested in are searching the catalog and viewing their account (renewals, check holds, etc.). While WordPress isn't technically designed to meet those needs, it can facilitate a user experience around those interactions that is welcoming and recognizable.

And indeed, JDL's website features both of these tasks prominently. A catalog search widget is in the header of every page, and there's a "My Account" link in the easy-to-find menu bar. Their theme's use of an image slider provides an easy way for the library to highlight upcoming events and library news. Once in the catalog, outside of WordPress, visitors will still see visual styles and elements very similar to what the library build in WordPress. Tying elements together like this can help hide the seams as patrons move between different systems.

Greenlee also has early plans to build a staff intranet, and is considering using WordPress for that project too. He notes that some groups use the multisite version of WordPress for this, allowing them to host their public website and private intranet together while keeping the two piles of content separate from each other. He also points to www.simpleintranet.org as a suite of WordPress plugins useful for this purpose.

Lastly, Greenlee highlights an important concern for using WordPress or any other content management system: patron privacy:

> I am wary of using WordPress for applications which might potentially involve storing private patron information, or personally identifiable employee information. And we're self-hosted. If our site was hosted elsewhere then it's almost a non-starter. We would have to seriously consider what data would be going in.

These potential issues are easy to address or avoid entirely, but only if you consider them early in your WordPress development process. Greenlee and JDL have obviously taken great care in crafting their site, and the end result is a wonderful experience for their patrons.

Durham County Library

Matthew Clobridge, library webmaster
Website: http://www.durhamcountylibrary.org

The Durham County Library (DCL) in Durham, North Carolina, has 160,000 library card holders. In a recent twelve-month period, their website served over 360,000 unique visitors and 2.9 million page views. Their users cover a broad range of demographics, tech-savviness, and access to technology.

Matthew Clobridge oversaw moving the Durham County Library website to WordPress in 2012. Their entire website is currently contained within WordPress (see figure 4.5), plus thirteen other "mini sites" including:

- Staff Intranet
- Summer Reading Program (http://durhamcountylibrary.org/summerreading)
- Durham Library Foundation (http://durhamlibraryfoundation.org)
- Durham Reads Together (http://durhamreadstogether.org)

Figure 4.5. Durham County Library Homepage

Like many of the library examples covered in this chapter, their previous website was done in HTML and not within any content management system. Durham County Library chose to move to WordPress for the content management features, customizability, and options to extend the platform with plugins. Their site is hosted at A Small Orange (http://www.asmallorange.com).

As sole maintainer of the site, Clobridge does the design and maintenance work himself. He uses the Canvas theme as the starting point for each of their sites, and creates child themes for each individual site to handle the customizations it needs (see chapter 5 for more on working with child themes, and why this is a good idea). His description of his favorite thing about working with WordPress is a great summary for why it's a good fit for libraries in general:

> I love that whatever I need a site to do, there is a way with Word-Press to make it happen. Many times I can do it with a free or inexpensive plugin, other times it's with some custom coding. But, there has never been a time when I had to say "no" to a feature request because WordPress couldn't handle it.

And the customization Clobridge and DCL have done is quite extensive. I'm particularly impressed and intrigued by their 2014 Summer Reading site, which included a number of quite complex features. Summer Reading Program participants could create an account, log in, and track their reading all within the bounds of this WordPress site. They earned points, which were also tracked by WordPress, and could trade them in for prizes.

This is an excellent example of a library going above and beyond using WordPress as a simple content management system. With some time and the freely available WordPress documentation, a single developer like Clobridge was able to build something unique and useful for his patrons. In this case, almost five thousand patrons used the site and provided tons of positive feedback. Clobridge plans to use the same system again in summer 2015, but enhanced with new features he's working on now.

Returning to the Durham County Library's main website, Clobridge spent about six months working with an internal web redesign committee to build the WordPress site. Like many libraries, their site has a number of contact forms. They use Gravity Forms, also seen in other case studies here, to manage forms like their online donation system. Clobridge notes that "if I can think it, Gravity Forms can do it. We purchased the developer license, which is $199 for the first year and about half that for renewals. It may seem like a lot, but it comes with all the Gravity Forms add-ons, priority support, and support for unlimited sites."

The Durham County Library's WordPress website is an excellent example of how even a small team can do extensive customization within WordPress and build amazing things. I look forward to following what they do with the software next!

K–12 LIBRARY AND MEDIA CENTER EXAMPLES

Holliston High School Library

MK Eagle, librarian
Website: http://libraryhhs.wordpress.com

Located in Holliston, Massachusetts, Holliston High School (HHS) Library serves over eight hundred students in grades 9–12. One hundred percent of their classrooms are connected to the Internet, and the district averages 2.4 students per computer. MK Eagle, librarian at the HHS Library, is the sole maintainer of her library's WordPress website (see figure 4.6).

HHS Library started using WordPress in 2009, making it one of the earliest library adopters of WordPress that I found while researching this book. And unlike most other case studies in this book, the HHS Library hosts their site at the free WordPress.com version of the service.

Remember that with the WordPress.com version of WordPress, you have a trade-off. It can be entirely free, but comes with reduced options for customization. Many potential users shy away from the free service because of those reductions, but I think the HHS Library makes a good counterpoint in favor of why this level of service can still be worth considering in some situations. Libraries of all types, not just K–12, often have limited financial and other resources available to them, and free or very cheap tools may be the only ones within reach. With a bit of

Figure 4.6.   Holliston High School Library Homepage

creativity and attention to detail, Eagle's work proves that a library can have a friendly, welcoming, attractive, and usable home on the web while functioning within the bounds of the free option.

Eagle has been using WordPress for various projects for a decade, and she brought that expertise to this project:

> I was already very familiar with WordPress, so I knew I'd be able to get a site up and running faster than if I had started with another platform. I think WordPress offers a great mix of templates and other ready-to-use content with editing and customization options for putting our unique spin on pages.

Because WordPress is so widely adopted on the web, it's very possible that your staff already has similar experience using it in different contexts. Ask around, you might be surprised to see who answers the call to help with a library WordPress site. Eagle was able to get the site "in skeleton form" up and running the very first day of her work on the project, and she's built content ever since.

HHS Library has a simple design that's very easy to navigate and read. It currently uses the San Kloud theme, but Eagle notes that she periodically changes themes to meet the organizational needs of the site. The site has a wonderful "Jump To" menu prominently displayed in the sidebar, pointing out commonly needed pages on the library's website.

This is a great idea on any website, whether it's constructed in WordPress or not. Commonly used resources and links should almost always be prominently displayed on a library's homepage.

WordPress makes it very easy to build this feature. In this case it's just one click to get to sections of the site like the calendar, catalog, citing sources, databases, and more. Library websites of all types can be complex animals, with deep structures and lots of pages full of information. Designing obvious and usable navigation through this quantity of *Pages* is difficult, and a "Jump To" list like this is a great way to address it.

The HHS Library homepage is in the WordPress blog format, with recent updates at the top and older ones as you scroll down. Eagle uses this to feature a regular "Friday Playlist" of songs on YouTube, a great way to get users engaged with and returning to the site.

The top navigation points students to resources for their classes, databases, citing sources, a calendar, and a list of recommended reading organized by genre. Sticking with a blog layout clearly doesn't mean you have to sacrifice complexity of content and navigation. Building all of this within the free WordPress.com offerings is both impressive and reproducible by other libraries.

Eagle is happy enough with using WordPress for her library that she's currently building another WordPress site for the Robert H. Adams Middle School (RAMS) Library. She describes her WordPress workflow in a way that probably sounds familiar to any librarian involved in multiple projects at the same time:

> I am the sole maintainer. I don't always edit content but I'm constantly using the website, as are teachers and students. If nothing else, all of our databases are linked from the website, so users have to visit the site to access them. Otherwise my workflow is identical to my other library tasks—I work on daily projects as well as longer-term goals as I can, but I'm constantly being pulled to other tasks and work with students and staff. WordPress' auto-save feature is a lifesaver!

Lastly, I love Eagle's advice for similar libraries thinking about using WordPress. She highlights the ability of a WordPress site to evolve as time rolls forward:

> Do it! And don't be afraid to tweak the site. I think a lot of teachers and librarians feel the need to master a technology tool or platform before they use it with students, but users today are used to seeing apps and sites in beta; they're accustomed to upgrades and fixes. Your site doesn't have to be perfect on day one.

SPECIAL LIBRARY EXAMPLES

Harvard-Smithsonian Center for Astrophysics John G. Wolbach Library

Christopher Erdmann, head librarian
Websites:

- Unified Astronomy Thesaurus: http://astrothesaurus.org/
- Galactic Gazette: http://altbibl.io/gazette/
- Liberact: http://altbibl.io/liberact/
- Data Scientist Training for Librarians: http://altbibl.io/dst4l/

Unlike other case studies presented here, the WordPress sites built by the Harvard-Smithsonian Center for Astrophysics John G. Wolbach Library are not general-purpose library websites. Instead, they are special-purpose sites designed to meet a specific purpose. To sum them up:

- The Unified Astronomy Thesaurus (http://astrothesaurus.org/), managed by the NASA Astrophysics Data System, seeks to unite "the existing divergent and isolated astronomy and astrophysics thesauri into a single high-quality, freely available open thesaurus formalizing astronomical concepts and their inter-relationships."
- Galactic Gazette (http://altbibl.io/gazette/) posts news from the staff at the Harvard-Smithsonian Center for Astrophysics.
- Liberact (http://altbibl.io/liberact/) was created for the Liberact Workshop on gesture-based systems for library settings, hosted at

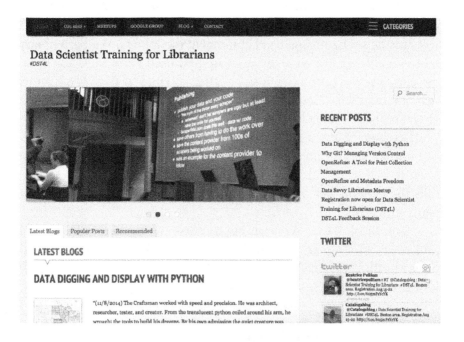

Figure 4.7.   Data Scientist Training for Libraries Homepage

Harvard in 2013. It now hosts the resulting content from the event.

- Data Scientist Training for Librarians (http://altbibl.io/dst4l/) manages the course, announcements, materials, and other information for this program.

These examples are important and relevant to all libraries, not just special libraries. They highlight WordPress' ability to be used for special-purpose projects and not necessarily as a replacement website for your library as a whole. This is similar to the way that the Durham County Library used WordPress (covered in a previous case study) to manage their summer reading program.

The sites maintained by this library are all worth a look for any library exploring WordPress. The examples cover the spectrum of many possible WordPress uses: straightforward blog-style news announcements, a publication meant for reference use by others, planning and archiving a conference-style event, and publishing resources related to a training program for librarians. No matter which type of library you work at, you can almost certainly find an example here relevant to a project coming your way.

Christopher Erdmann, head librarian at the John G. Wolbach library told me a bit about how they've set up and used WordPress for these projects. They've been using it since 2012, and picked WordPress for its "ease of use, management of roles, responsiveness on devices, and large library of themes and plugins."

They host all these sites with Dreamhost, and got the first one up and running in just three to five days. Erdmann says they chose Dreamhost "so that we can respond to needs that happen on the fly." And he calls the content management system "a perfect fit for our [and] the patrons' needs."

Again, the John G. Wolbach library's use of WordPress for special projects is an example relevant throughout the library world. I'm impressed with their creative thinking of how to use WordPress, and look forward to seeing their upcoming projects.

Vermont Library Association

Jessamyn West, webmaster
Website: http://www.vermontlibraries.org

The Vermont Library Association (VLA) moved their entire website into WordPress in November 2007, making them the earliest library adopter of WordPress that I found while researching these case studies (see figure 4.8). Their previous library website was static HTML, and all content was maintained by one person.

Jessamyn West, webmaster for the site, describes what VLA was looking for when moving away from a plain HTML site:

- A place for the organization and various committees to archive documents.
- A place to have public-facing policies and documents.
- A place for people to get information about the organization.
- A place for people to be able to interact with the organization.
- A place for news and events and advocacy.

They ultimately chose WordPress because "it was the one we had the most experience with, it was free and it was flexible so that we could

Figure 4.8.   Vermont Library Association Homepage

use plugins and add-ons and get help from the wealth of information online about it. I've used it for managing my own blogs and I've been impressed by the user community and how easy it is to find someone else who is trying to answer the same questions that you are."

VLA currently uses the Vantage Premium theme, which is responsive.

I love that this site uses WordPress' blog features on the front page to highlight both institutional business and the work of libraries around the state of Vermont. The institutional business-related functions for members, sections, and committees are still very present on the site, but as a front door the homepage is well-designed and welcoming.

West's favorite thing about WordPress is mine too: "I can find the answer to any tech support question I have just by Googling effectively." The amount of information online about using and troubleshooting WordPress is amazingly rich and helpful, and nudges it above many other content management systems.

I also like that VLA is open to swapping features in and out on their site as necessary. For example, they used a plugin called Milestone to display a countdown to their conference in a fun and simple way. They also constructed a job posting section of the site, all built within Word-Press.

Lastly, West highlights one of the major things VLA likes about using WordPress over a plain HTML site: "I think a lot of people really liked the 'send your stuff to one person and they update it and you never have to think about it' system, but that doesn't really work well in an all-volunteer organization."

With WordPress, VLA lets content creators have direct access to the *Pages* they're responsible for. This helps them keep their site current, timely, and informative for their members across the state.

Recollection Wisconsin

Emily Pfotenhauer, Recollection Wisconsin program manager, Wisconsin Library Services
Website: http://www.recollectionwisconsin.org

Emily Pfotenhauer, Recollection Wisconsin program manager, describes her user population simply and broadly: "We consider our user population to be the entire state of Wisconsin."

Recollection Wisconsin serves as a central collection of resources digitized by libraries, archives, museum, and historical societies across the state. Unsurprisingly for a site all about digitized images and other media, they make excellent use of WordPress's multimedia features and options (see figure 4.9).

The homepage features a rotating list of recent stories, and each story is a combination of text and media. A simple header navigation menu invites users to search, browse, share, or teach. The impressively detailed search options are all built entirely within WordPress, and then direct the user to external websites to view details about each item in the collections. Pfotenhauer describes their overall web strategy broken into three parts:

- "WordPress is the home for our program blog, online exhibits and other interpretive materials, and guidelines and documentation for program participants."
- "The aggregated database of more than two hundred thousand digital objects is hosted and managed by UW-Madison."
- "An extensive social media presence (Facebook, Twitter, Tumblr, and Pinterest) brings our partners' digital materials to a broader audience."

Figure 4.9.   Recollection Wisconsin Homepage

As you've seen in other case studies and throughout this book, it isn't at all unusual for WordPress to cover something less than the entirety of a library's website. Your catalog, databases, and other content often have to live elsewhere. But with a little work like what Recollection Wisconsin has done, WordPress can be the glue that ties those sections together into one cohesive look and feel for your web presence.

Launched in February 2013, the WordPress portion of the site was part of a rebranding for the program with a new name and logo. The previous site was in plain HTML, and WordPress was recommended to them as a solution requiring minimal IT support. Pfotenhauer also had some WordPress experience from a previous project. She worked with two designers to create the site. While the design process took about eight months, the actual construction of the site itself took just a few days. Be sure to allow plenty of time for planning out your site, not just implementing it in WordPress!

Recollection Wisconsin uses a variety of plugins, including:

- Custom Sidebars, to create separate navigation for different parts of the site.
- SliderPRO, to create some of their image slideshows.
- MailChimp Campaign Archive, to automatically embed links to all of the email newsletters sent using MailChimp.
- Public Post Preview, to generate temporary links for unpublished content. Recollection Wisconsin often works with guest curators, so this allows Pfotenhauer to send them a preview link without having to give them an account to access the WordPress admin options.

Pfotenhauer's advice for libraries considering WordPress is "don't be afraid to test things out!":

> If I need a new functionality, I just search the plugin directory, test out a few different plugins and then implement the one that works best for what I need. For example, we don't have a responsive theme so I needed to figure out a simple option to make the site more mobile-friendly. I think I tried out about six different mobile plugins before I found one that I liked, but it was really easy and quick to test them because you just have to activate and deactivate the plugin.

Recollection Wisconsin also gets value out of looking at analytics on their site. They can see what search terms bring people to the site, and their engagement numbers have improved over the previous version of the site.

5

STEP-BY-STEP LIBRARY PROJECTS FOR WORDPRESS

It's time to dive in! Now that your site is up and running and you've seen some examples of how great library websites can use WordPress, you're ready to start customizing and tweaking your site to best serve your users. This chapter covers:

- How to Install and Use Common Plugins
- How to Install and Customize a Theme
- How to Build an Exhibit to Display an Image Collection
- How to Analyze and Manage Your Content in WordPress
- How to Create Re-Usable Chunks of Text With Shortcodes
- How to Build a Professional Library Website

HOW TO INSTALL AND USE COMMON PLUGINS

You don't need to have even a bit of programming experience to customize WordPress to better meet the needs of your library users. Installing plugins is a straightforward process, letting you point and click your way to a more functional and beautiful site. This section will show you how to install a plugin, before outlining how to install and set up five common and useful plugins on your site:

- *Jetpack,* a bundle of useful enhancements and tweaks

- *Akismet*, for protection from spam
- *Formidable*, an easy way to create interactive forms on your site
- *Press Permit*, which allows you to create custom access levels for different staff users
- *Wordfence* security, which provides a simple and strong first line of defense for your site

Once you've got the hang of these five, you'll have the skills to install and use any plugin you want.

Because the WordPress.com version of WordPress doesn't let you install your own plugins, this project assumes you're using the hosted version of WordPress from WordPress.org.

Installing a Plugin

Recent versions of WordPress have made great strides toward an improved plugin installation experience. You can now install most plugins without the need to manually upload files or tweak any code. Here's the basic steps, which are repeatable for any plugin:

1. Log in to your WordPress site's administration panel.
2. Hold your mouse over "Plugins" in the black bar on the left.
3. Click "Add New."
4. Search for the name of the plugin you want to install.
5. Click the "Install Now" button below the plugin's name.
6. Once installation is complete, click the "Activate Plugin" link.
7. Click the "Settings" link in your list of installed plugins to configure it. Note that not all plugins will have settings available to you.

Jetpack

Jetpack lets you bring some of the excellent features added to the WordPress.com version of the software to your very own self-hosted installation! Among its many features, Jetpack adds:

- Usage statistics about your site.
- Social network enabled comments.
- Advanced search options on your site.

- Easy integration of directly uploaded videos.
- Alerts if your site goes down.
- Many more! See the full list at http://wordpress.org/plugins/jetpack.

Installation and Activation

Following the instructions above, search for and install the Jetpack plugin. As always, don't forget to activate it! To get the full power of the Jetpack plugin, you need to connect it to a free WordPress.com account. This might seem confusing since you're not using WordPress.com to host your site—you're running it yourself! But for features like the built-in statistics, Jetpack still relies on some of the underlying infrastructure that powers WordPress.com. You should see a big green "Connect to WordPress.com" banner at the top of your admin screen. Click that button, and log in with a WordPress.com account (if you don't already have one, you can create one from the login page too). You just have to do this once, and never again.

After logging in, you'll see a helpful tour of some of Jetpack's major features. There's also now a new Jetpack item in your black WordPress administrative menu on the left side of the screen. Click it, then the "Settings" link that appears below it to enable and disable different features of Jetpack.

Basic Use and Configuration

You can explore many of the features Jetpack offers at your leisure, but I want to highlight the Statistics in particular. Look again in the black admin menu on the left side of your screen.

You can click on "Site Stats" to get an overview of how many visitors there have been to your site recently.

Clicking on "Omnisearch" instead takes you to a search box that looks through every piece of content you've ever added to your site: *Pages*, *Posts*, Comments, Media, etc. Even the broader repository of plugins returns results. This is a powerful tool for managing content on your site.

If bandwidth limits or speed are a concern for your site, consider enabling the Photon portion of Jetpack. If you use it, WordPress will host your site's images for you on their speedy and well-maintained servers free of charge.

Other features of Jetpack may be slightly redundant when compared to other plugins covered in this chapter. For example, while the Jetpack Contact Form feature is nice, building forms with the Formidable plugin (covered later) is more flexible and useful in the long run. And if you've already chosen a responsive theme to make your site look good on mobile devices, then the Jetpack Mobile Theme is redundant too.

But spend some time exploring all the options listed in the Jetpack settings screen. You might be surprised by how useful some of them are, particularly for promoting and publicizing your content via e-mail and social media. Many of these features would be difficult to accomplish otherwise, or would require installing a whole host of separate plugins. But Jetpack does it all at once!

Akismet

If you plan to have any enabled comment forms on your WordPress website, Akismet is highly recommended. While it has a free version which is fine to get started, Akismet will cost you $5 per month for the version that's licensed to use on a final version of your site. In my view this is a steal; WordPress sites can get hit with comment spam, and without Akismet you'll find yourself doing a lot of extra clicking to clean things up.

Installation and Activation

Akismet is also the perfect first plugin to play with—because it's already installed! Akismet is so important that it has been included with every version of WordPress since way back in version 2.0. So you can actually skip the numbered installation steps above in this case. Simply click on the "Plugins" section of your WordPress administrative menu and you'll see it listed.

While the plugin is pre-installed, you still need to activate it. Activation is the final step in adding a plugin to your site. Because plugins can, in very rare cases, conflict with each other or not work the way you expect, activating or deactivating a plugin is a quick way to test things on your site without the need to fully uninstall a plugin. The "Plugins" section of the menu is where you can go to flip this switch. In this case, just click "Activate" next to Akismet.

Basic Use and Configuration

Akismet requires a little bit more configuration at this point. You should see a large green bar across the top of your screen, as in figure 5.1.

This process might look complicated, but I promise it's actually pretty straightforward and only needs to be done once. Here's what you need to do:

1. Click the "Activate" button.
2. Click "Get Your API Key." A new webpage will open.
3. On the new webpage, click "Get an Akismet API Key."
4. Fill in the form with your information, and click "Sign Up."
5. Select the free Personal account level and continue.
6. Now you finally have your Akismet API key! It looks like a bunch of random numbers and letters.
7. Copy and paste your key back into WordPress, in the "Manually Enter an API Key" box and click "Use This Key."
8. That's it! Good job, you never have to go through this process again.
9. Your WordPress site is now protected from spammy comments!

Note that while the free version of Akismet is fine for experimentation, if you're going to use it on your final site you should go back and switch to the $5 per month plan. This will make sure your site is covered under the correct licensing category. If you don't plan on allowing visitors to comment on your site, it's perfectly okay to skip using Akismet entirely.

Figure 5.1.   Akismet Configuration Link

Formidable

If you have any kind of interactive elements on your site, Formidable is a must-have plugin. Formidable lets you create forms with a simple and powerful drag-and-drop interface. Like most of WordPress' features, you can create complex forms and workflows without writing a single line of code. Formidable not only helps you create the form itself, but also makes it easy to manage the responses on the back end. The Formidable website correctly notes that "you can create completely custom forms in less time than you spend brewing your morning coffee."

The basic version of Formidable is free, and that is the one we'll be looking at here. There's also an upgraded version available for a one-time purchase of $47, which adds some extra field types and some more options for form management. But the free version is still extremely useful, and should meet most libraries' needs.

Installation and Activation

To install Formidable, follow the instructions at the start of this chapter. The plugin you're looking for is listed in the plugin directory as "Formidable Forms." Don't forget to click "Activate Plugin" once it's installed!

After installing the plugin, you should see an extra entry (labeled "Formidable") in the left-side black menu of your administrative interface. Click that link to go to Formidable and see what other options are available to you.

Basic Use and Configuration

After clicking "Formidable" in the black administrative menu, you'll see the options to build a form. To create a new form, click "Add New" near the top of your screen next to the "Forms" label. Now you're given two options: Start with a pre-built Contact Us form, or work on a blank form from scratch. Let's look at the pre-built option; below the "Contact Us" drop-down menu, click the "Create" button.

After just that one click, you'll see a standard "Contact Us" form with fields like name, e-mail, and message.

Look down near the bottom of the form, where there's even a built-in captcha. By asking your users to type some words, Formidable drastically cuts down on any spam submitted through your form. There's a

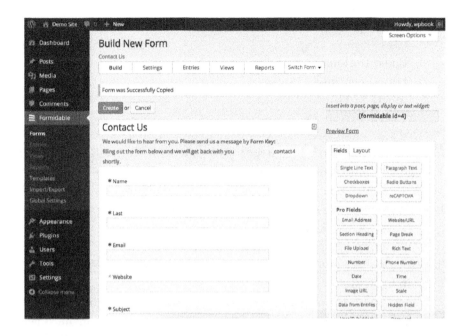

Figure 5.2. Formidable Configuration Options

note below the captcha about some extra configuration necessary to make it work—don't worry, we'll come back to that later.

If this form meets your needs, great! If not, just click on anything you want to change (see figure 5.2). Clicking a label like "Name" or "Subject" lets you edit it. Or you can click on any of the text boxes to reveal extra options. Here you can quickly change the position of a label, the size of the text box, and make other customizations. You can also click the star next to a label to toggle whether or not that field is required when submitting the form. To change the order of fields, hold your mouse over the one you want to move. On the right side of the highlighted box, a cross icon will appear. Click that icon and drag the field to wherever you want it on the form.

To add a new field entirely, look in the box of field types on the right side of your screen. Simply click and drag the field type you want onto your form. Once you've dropped it there, you can configure and label it the same way you did above. With the free version of Formidable, you have access to six field types:

1. Single Line Text;
2. Paragraph Text;
3. Checkboxes;
4. Radio Buttons;
5. Dropdown; and
6. reCAPTCHA.

That's an impressive list, with which you can build almost any form imaginable. The extra field types you gain with the paid version of Formidable are listed below those six on the form creation screen. While they add some nice options like a pre-configured e-mail address field and some extra layout options, the six included free ones are still quite powerful and flexible enough to create most forms.

Once you've got the form organized and labeled the way you want it, look for the horizontal menu bar near the top of your screen. You can see it in figure 5.2.

Click "Settings" in that menu. Here you can change things like the text displayed on your submit button and the confirmation message users see after submitting your form. If you have Akismet installed for spam protection as discussed earlier in this chapter, you can even enable it here to check your forms for spammy submissions!

One of the most important settings screens to check here is the "E-mails" tab. Here you configure the e-mail that gets sent when your form is submitted. This is useful not only for sending a notification to your website administrator or other staff member, but also for sending a confirmation to the user if your form handled event registration or something similar. Once you're done changing these settings, click "Update" at the bottom of the screen.

Look back at the horizontal menu in figure 5.2 above. The third item there, "Entries," is also important. This is where you can see all submissions to your form. No need to hold onto all those e-mails. You always have a spreadsheet-style layout of all form entries saved here for later reference or statistical analysis. Right now you won't see any entries, because nobody's filled out your form yet. Let's fix that.

Now you've got a great Contact Us form, but it's not displayed anywhere on your site. Go back to the *Pages* section of your black WordPress menu bar, and add a new *Page* called Contact Us. You'll now see a button above the main text edit box labeled "Add Form." Click that, and pick the form you want from the list of all available forms. Click "Insert Form," and that's it! You'll see a line of code added to your page—that's what tells WordPress to display your form there. You don't need to write the code yourself, you just need to know that this is what it does. If you click "Preview" or "Publish," you'll see your Contact Us form in all its glory. Go ahead and try it out, submit something. Then go back to the "Entries" menu in figure 5.2 and take a look at the nice useful view Formidable gives you of your saved information. Check for the e-mail you set up too.

Congratulations, you have a fully functioning customized form. You can now go back and create any others you need for tasks like an event registration, room reservation, book purchase request, or anything else you can think of.

Advanced Configuration

Earlier I mentioned that getting the captcha field to work in Formidable takes a little bit of extra setup. This is completely optional, but if you want to get it working it's not too difficult.

Go back to your form in Formidable, as if you were going to edit it, and way down at the bottom, below the captcha, click the "Set Up" link that's in red text. You'll end up at a general settings page for Formidable, which includes a section labeled "reCaptcha." You'll need to enter both a public and private key. Getting those keys is a completely free process, and you can get yours at http://www.google.com/recaptcha/admin. Once you have them, come back to this settings page and paste them in. Now the captcha field will appear on your form and help filter out spam.

Press Permit

Sometimes you don't want every library staff member who works on your website to have access to the whole thing. Limiting a user's edit access to just the pages relevant to their work both makes the WordPress interface simpler for them and prevents accidental edits or deletions to pages outside the scope of their job. While WordPress gives you some basic permission levels by default (covered back in chapter 3), a plugin called Press Permit will give you much more robust options for assigning permissions to users.

While I've tried to focus this chapter on freely available plugins and features, using Press Permit to limit page access in this way is an exception. It's a feature you'll need to pay for. To use Press Permit on your single website, you'll be charged $55. In my opinion, this cost is justified. I spent hours researching and trying to find a free alternative to highlight instead. Every option I found either didn't work, was extremely confusing, or was no longer actively maintained. If your website has no budget for plugins, you can look into Role Scoper instead at http://wordpress.org/plugins/role-scoper. It was the best alternative to Press Permit I found, but I still believe Press Permit is a superior option and worth the cost.

Installation and Activation

By now you're an expert at installing plugins. Follow the instructions from the beginning of this section again, this time searching for Press Permit Core. And once again, don't forget to activate the plugin after you install it. You'll also need to install and activate the PP Collaborative Editing Pack plugin. This second plugin isn't in the standard plugin directory, and you'll only receive it (with clear installation instructions too) after paying for Press Permit.

Once both components of Press Permit are installed, you'll see a new "Permissions" link in your familiar black WordPress administrative menu. Click it to see what options and settings are available. Press Permit is an extremely powerful plugin, and we'll be looking at the basic settings and options. There's so much more on each page that can't be covered in the space allowed here, so feel free to come back later and experiment more with the highly customizable permission options.

Basic Use and Configuration

Press Permit works by creating a group with the desired access permissions and then assigning your users to that group. By default, before Press Permit is installed, WordPress lets you assign a user to one of five groups:

1. Author: Can manage and publish only their own pages and posts.
2. Subscriber: Can manage only their profile options. No access to pages or posts.

3. Contributor: Can write and manage their own pages and posts as drafts, but can't publish them to the live site.
4. Editor: Can publish anyone's posts and pages to the live site.
5. Administrator: Has access to all content and options on the site.

These are useful, but in a multi-user situation it can be nice to have a little more fine-tuned control over what content each staff member can access and edit. This is especially true on larger sites, where a user might not need or want access to every *Page*. Let's create a new group, assign a user, and give them some example permissions.

Before we go any further, you'll need at least one new user and a handful of *Pages* to experiment with. If you haven't already, go create a new user (under the "Users" section of the black WordPress menu bar) and a few *Pages* to play with. They can even be blank *Pages* for now, that's perfectly OK. When you create the extra user, make sure to set them as an Editor.

Once you've got those pieces set up, let's look at the new options Press Permit makes available for us. In the black WordPress menu bar on the left side of your screen, click "Permissions." You'll see a list of the default WordPress groups, a description of what they are, and some other metadata. If we want to limit a user's editor access to just one page instead of all pages, none of these options really meet our needs.

Press Permit has many ways to add this kind of restriction, such as creating new roles and assigning various permissions to those roles. If you have a large website with tons of *Pages*, that's probably the way to go and is a bit easier to maintain. But for a small site or just starting out with WordPress and Press Permit, it's very easy to deal with each *Page* on a case-by-case basis instead. Let's take a look at how that works.

The test user you created above is an Editor, which means they have access to all the *Pages* on the site. If you want to restrict that access, click on the "Users" section of the black WordPress admin menu. Find the user you want to edit permissions for, and click their name.

Now, scroll down and look for the "Custom User Permissions" section. It should be a box with a light blue background. Inside that box, click the "Customize This User Directly" link (see figure 5.3).

If it isn't selected already, click the "Add Exceptions" tab near the top of the page. This will display a series of dropdown menus you can use to set which *Pages* the user has access to. You can try different

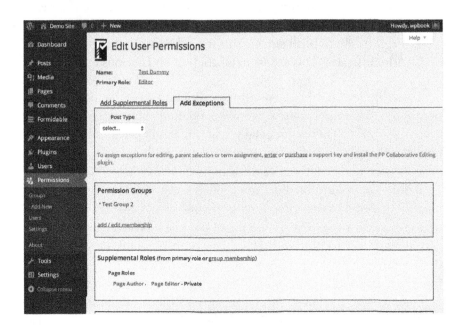

Figure 5.3.   Press Permit Configuration Options

combinations of settings to achieve different effects and access levels, but here are some recommendations:

- Post Type: Page.
- Post Operation: Edit.
- Adjustment: Only these.
- Check off both "Selected Pages" and "sub-Page of."

Once those settings are chosen, you simply have to check off boxes for the *Pages* you want this user to have access to. With these settings, they'll also be able to access any child *Page* of what you check here.

For example, if you have a Young Adult page, which in turn has a handful of child pages, and you want the young adult librarian to have access to all of them, just check off the main Young Adult *Page*. As long as the "Adjustment" box was set to "Only These" above, their account can now access only this subset of pages.

Press Permit is a powerful tool, and worth the modest one-time purchase. As you've seen here, you don't have to drive yourself crazy exploring every nook and cranny of the features it offers. But of all the plugins in this book, Press Permit is probably the one you'll want to spend the most time experimenting and configuring. I constantly discover features in it that make my job easier!

Wordfence Security

If you've been following along with this book's recommendations for configuring and setting up your WordPress site, you're well on your way to a safe and secure installation. But it never hurts to be prepared and have an extra layer of security involved. While larger libraries and institutions may have the luxury of a full-time staff member to watch for issues like server and software security, smaller libraries and personal users have other options that fill in the gaps nicely. One of these is the Wordfence plugin.

Wordfence guards against attempts to hack your site, both via guessed passwords and sneakier attacks targeting the underlying source code. The plugin monitors activity on your site, constantly analyzing it for suspicious activity.

Installation and Activation

Wordfence is in the plugin directory just like every other plugin listed here. Install and activate it as usual. After installation, you'll be prompted to enter an e-mail address. This address is important: it's where Wordfence will send you security alerts and related updates. Enter it, click the "Get Alerted" button, and then follow the prompted Wordfence feature tour. It does quite a nice job of walking you through the features and settings.

Basic Use and Configuration

After installation, you'll see a new Wordfence section of your black admin menu. Click on it to see all the options and features available to you. The "Scan" section lets you do an in-depth search for security issues on your site. The free version of Wordfence skips a few of the finer details of the scan, but still checks for a wide array of common red flags. Give it a try—see if anything pops up! Wordfence will also suggest solutions to any problems encountered.

The "Live Traffic" section of Wordfence can be fascinating. It provides a live view of any attack attempts against your site. Don't panic if you see a bunch of them—WordPress itself is built to handle these attempts as long as you keep it up to date. But a quick glance at this section for even a moderately popular site can reinforce just how important security is for WordPress.

The "Advanced Blocking" section provides an easy way to block IP address ranges from accessing your site—useful if you are being flooded with non-legitimate site requests.

Explore the "Options" section of Wordfence too. Here you can configure which e-mail alerts you'll receive, plus a number of other features to enable or disable. I particularly recommend looking at the "Login Security Options" of this page. It lets you lock out users after a given number of login failures or lost password attempts, and prevents them from trying again. Although you should of course have strong passwords to begin with, this can help prevent anyone from guessing random words as a way to log in. On my personal WordPress site, I have Wordfence set to e-mail me every time an administrator logs in. I'm the only administrator on the site, so if I ever get an e-mail that wasn't generated by my login I know something's up.

Wordfence won't necessarily prevent all attacks against your site, but it does add a valuable set of security tools to your arsenal. It's hard to be secure if you aren't watching what's happening on your site, and Wordfence makes it very easy to keep that eye out.

HOW TO INSTALL AND CUSTOMIZE A THEME

Back in chapter 2 you learned the basics of how to select and install a WordPress theme. Remember that a theme controls the look and feel of your website: layout, some graphics, and styles are all contained in the theme. While you could do all this customization yourself, themes deliver it all in one neat package. And to make it even better, you don't have to write any code to use them. Installing most themes is a strictly point and click event. Themes have updates released from time to time, which might add a new feature, fix compatibility issues with new browsers, or fix a bug.

More than 2,500 themes are currently available in the official Word-Press.org theme directory (http://wordpress.org/themes), with countless others also available on other sites. While many themes are free, others do have a cost associated with them. But most of the time you can find a free theme that will meet your library's needs.

Still, what if that theme isn't quite perfect? It's not uncommon to make slight tweaks to a theme. Maybe it's 99 percent what you want, but you wish the links were blue instead of the theme's default green color. That's easy enough to change with a slight settings tweak, but what happens when an update for your theme is released? If you haven't set your theme up right, it might just overwrite those changes you so carefully made.

In this section we'll review how to choose and install a theme, and then cover how to use child themes to avoid losing your beautiful theme tweaks.

Finding a Theme

As mentioned before, the main WordPress theme directory at http://wordpress.org/themes is a rich pool with thousands of options to pick from. Beyond the lists of most popular and newest themes, you can also filter through the themes for features and layouts you want. You can filter by features like the dominant color, number of columns, whether it's responsive, and the customization options it offers. But which of these criteria are truly important?

Choosing a Responsive Theme

Even if you don't filter the theme list by any other options, I recommend you set the "Layout" options to "Responsive-Layout." Picking a responsive theme will ensure that your site displays well across all devices and screen sizes with no extra work.

Once upon a time (ok, maybe just a couple of years ago) making a content management system like WordPress play nicely across desktops, laptops, tablets, and phones was a daunting task. It often took managing a pile of plugins and other customizations to make sure users had a good experience using your site on the device of their choice. It was very easy to miss a device category, and testing across every option was extremely hard. Responsive design, in a nutshell, is a type of design that automatically scales nicely across all of those different screen types. If done well, your content will neatly reorganize itself into narrower columns without forcing anyone to do annoying extra scrolling or to be cut off from the content they want entirely.

For an example of a responsively designed site, take a look at UNC Library's site (http://library.unc.edu) or the Children's Museum of Pittsburgh (http://pittsburghkids.org). Load them up on the device of your choice and see how they look. Or on your desktop, just resize your browser window to see content rearrange itself on the fly.

The takeaway here is that choosing a responsive theme will save you a bunch of work. So check off that filter box in the giant themes list. You'll still be left with hundreds of options, so don't worry that there won't be much in the way of variety.

You're certainly welcome to explore other non-responsive themes too, but keep in mind that you might make some extra work for yourself if you pick one.

If you'd like to learn more about responsive design, see Jason Clark's book in this series: *Responsive Web Design in Practice*.

Other Places to Find Themes

While the official WordPress theme directory is certainly extensive, it isn't exhaustive. These are some other theme repositories you can browse around:

- www.Themeforest.net
- www.ElegantThemes.com
- www.Themify.me
- www.Themeroulette.com

Installing and Configuring Your Theme

Once you've picked out a theme, it's time to go back into your Word-Press admin options. In that black bar on the left side of the screen, click "Appearance." In the sub-options that appear below that link, click "Themes." Next, click the "Add New" button at the top of the screen.

You can browse and filter themes here too, just like in the main repository. Or search for the name of the theme you want to install in the upper right corner. Hold your mouse over any of the results from your search, and you'll see a "Details & Preview" button. This is an extremely useful feature, allowing you to see what your site might look like in this theme before applying it. If you like it, just click "Install." Congratulations, you've added a theme.

If the theme you want didn't show up in the search results, or if you bought a premium theme directly from a creator, look at any documentation that they provided with the theme. It will usually outline exactly how to install it. Often this involves using an FTP program to manually add the files to the wp-content/themes folder on your server. Once uploaded, the theme will appear in your administrative "Themes" list and you can activate it from there.

Your theme might look a little blank or uninspired. Some, like the popular Responsive theme (it's both functionally responsive as covered above and is actually named "Responsive") are designed to be a blank slate for you to build on top of. Others have a more established identity immediately after being installed. Whether you pick a blank or more developed theme will depend on your own knowledge and skills in web design—CSS in particular. But never be afraid to stand on the shoulders of an existing theme—take advantage of the work others have done.

Exactly what point and click customization options you have at this point will vary from theme to theme. Some have built-in options to upload your own header image, for example, or you may be able to make some color choices from drop-down menus. To see what's available to you, go back to the "Appearance" section of your admin menu. Click "Themes," then hold your mouse over your active theme. If your theme has options, you'll see a blue "Customize" button appear.

In this "Customize" section you can make basic changes like setting your Title and Tagline, changing some colors and images, and often selecting your navigation style or widget layout. Again, this list will vary a bit from theme to theme. But you can often make surprisingly complicated layout changes in this simple menu, so spend some time exploring whatever options are available to you. Don't worry about messing anything up at this point, since you can always just reinstall the theme and start from a clean slate.

Working With Widgets in Your Theme

Many WordPress themes let you work with widgets. Widgets are small chunks of content that you can position in various parts of your theme's design. A widget might contain a search box for your site, links to archived pages, a calendar of events, a form, or a simple block of text that you want displayed across your site on multiple *Pages*. Plugins can often provide you with a new widget to display on your site. For example, the popular Jetpack plugin, discussed earlier in this chapter, includes a widget to display your Twitter feed in a box on your site.

Each theme provides different widgets and different places to display them. Each display location is called a sidebar. Each sidebar can contain multiple widgets, and each widget can go in multiple sidebars. To see what widgets and sidebars you have available thanks to your chosen plugins and theme, go back to the "Appearance" section of your admin menu and then click "Widgets."

In the left column of this page you'll see a list of the widgets you have available to you. The right column shows the sidebars available to display widgets in. One or more of your sidebars may already contain widgets. If you want to remove them, simply click and drag them out of the sidebar box. To add a widget to a sidebar, do just the opposite: click and drag one from the left column into your chosen sidebar. These changes are instant on your live site, with no need to click a save button.

Some widgets may need further configuration. The Twitter widget, which I mentioned before and comes included with the Jetpack plugin, will need to be told which Twitter account to display. To display options for a widget in a sidebar, click the small triangle icon on the right side of the widget's label. Any option it has will expand out, such as the required Twitter ID in this case.

I want to especially point out the simple text widget. This widget is often overlooked, but can be extremely useful in both small and large sites. It lets you display plain text or HTML in the sidebar by simply filling in a text box. That's an extremely easy way to make sure an important bit of content appears on every page of your site. For example, you could use the text widget to display your library's hours or an emergency closing notice. By updating that content in this one place, it gets pushed out across your entire site. This feature can be made even more powerful if you mix it with using shortcodes, covered later in this chapter.

Widgets are a sometimes underused feature of WordPress, but they show off exactly what a content management system is supposed to do—make managing and updating your content easier.

Advanced Theme Customization

If you're lucky, you found a theme close to your needs and were able to hammer it into shape with the built-in customization options. But what if that didn't quite get you where you want to be? The great thing about WordPress is that the underlying code, whether it be the CMS itself or the theme sitting on top, is entirely open source. You can peek at the PHP code and modify it to your heart's content.

Maybe your theme contains the page or post author's name, and you want to hide it. Or what if you really want to change the color of something, but that isn't an option in the theme's settings? That's when we need to look at the code a bit. WordPress does its best to make this easy—there's no need to fire up a separate program to edit the code. You can do it all right in your browser.

Go back to the "Appearance" section of your black menu bar. There are two sections relevant to customization here: Edit CSS and Editor.

Clicking "Edit CSS" will let you access your site's underlying layout code. Learning CSS is outside the scope of this book, but the basics are also very easy to pick up. This section is where you change the color or size of pretty much anything in your theme, plus make many other kinds of changes. If you'd like to learn CSS, I recommend free online tutorials like those at http://www.codecademy.com/ or http://www.w3schools.com/css/. If you've already got some CSS chops, feel free to hack away at the code here.

Clicking "Editor" instead gets you to the underlying PHP code of your theme. While editing the CSS would let us change the look and feel of a theme, editing the PHP gives us an even deeper level of control. You should see a list of templates on the right side of the page. Clicking any of them will open that PHP file for editing. Tweaking themes this way is again out of the scope of this book. But you shouldn't be intimidated, since sometimes this is the only way to make the change you want. Tons of relevant documentation is available in the WordPress codex at http://codex.wordpress.org/, and making simple tweaks like removing an author's name is a pretty straightforward process.

But no matter which method of editing this code you go with, there's one very important fact to keep in mind. Without some simple preparation, your work could be wiped out the next time your theme gets an update. The theme coders don't know about the awesome changes you made, so their new files won't contain them. But luckily there's a pretty easy way around this problem: Child Themes.

Using a Child Theme

By now you've picked a theme, installed it, and even made some customizations. And you definitely want to make sure those finely tuned changes you made aren't wiped out the next time your theme updates. By creating a Child Theme before you make your customizations, the impact of this problem can be minimized.

In a Child Theme, you create a set of changes that override the underlying original theme. When WordPress needs to load a file from your theme, it checks first to see if you've provided a tweaked version. If you did, then it loads your version. If not, then it pulls up the original theme instead.

Creating a Child Theme used to take some tedious coding and file manipulation via FTP. But not anymore—as with most WordPress tasks, there's a plugin for it.

Go back to the "Plugins" section of your site and search for a plugin called "One-Click Child Theme." Install and activate it as usual, and then click on "Appearance" in your admin menu. In the list of links that appears below it, click on the new "Child Theme" link. Give your theme a name and description in the form, then click "Create Child."

The plugin will do all the file manipulation work for you, and then automatically switch your theme to your shiny new Child Theme. Now you can customize to your heart's content, while being confident that an unexpected theme update won't wipe out your work (see figure 5.4). For more on working with Child Themes, check out the resources listed in the section titled Recommended Reading.

HOW TO BUILD AN EXHIBIT TO DISPLAY AN IMAGE COLLECTION

So far this book has focused primarily on using WordPress to organize and display traditional text-based content. But what if you have grander aspirations for your site? WordPress thankfully does more than text. Chapter 3 touched briefly on some of the options for media management available in WordPress, but here we'll look more in depth. Specif-

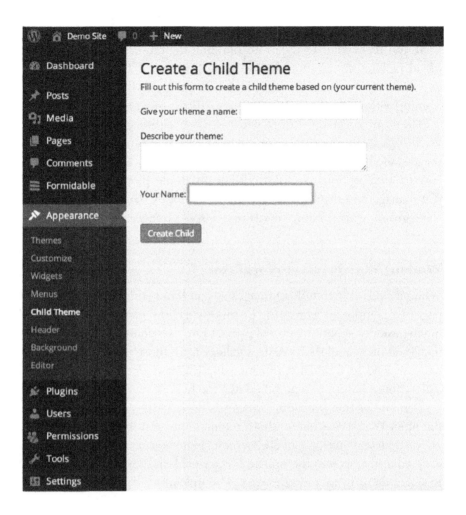

Figure 5.4.   Child Theme Configuration Options

ically, this section will detail some options you have for displaying an exhibit of an image collection. This kind of project can be useful for a number of purposes, including:

- featuring images from special collections
- showing off a recent renovation or new branch
- posting photos of a library event
- a gallery of your staff members, putting faces with your library's valuable work

• a collection of notable book covers from your collection

If you truly want to dive into building digital collections, I recommend picking up another volume from this series: *Digital Collections and Exhibits* by Juan Denzer. But this project will get you up and running with all the exhibit options WordPress provides.

There are so many things you can do with images in WordPress! We'll look at the built-in photo exhibit and gallery options that come pre-installed with WordPress. Next we'll move on to some image-focused theme options, and lastly point out some plugins that can help you manage and display your images more easily. But first, let's revisit some groundwork on how WordPress handles images.

Working With Media in WordPress

While it's possible to upload images as you build your gallery or display page, I recommend against it. From a workflow perspective, I find it much easier to separate out this project into two phases: upload all your images at once, and then create a gallery from those photos. Mixing the two can lead to a bit of confusion, duplicated image files, and a final gallery that's harder to maintain down the line.

Remember that uploading images is done in the "Media" section of the main WordPress black admin menu. Click that link, then the "Add New" button at the top of the screen. Now you can simply drag and drop your images into the upload box, or click the "Select Files" button to select them from a file browser. The upload itself shouldn't take too much time.

Now you'll see your images as thumbnails across the lower portion of the screen. It's tempting to move on at this point and jump straight into building a gallery. But take a few minutes here, indulge your librarian instincts, and add a little metadata to the files first. It'll make management of these images later so much easier. It's not uncommon to stumble across old images in WordPress months or years down the line, and have no memory of what they were originally uploaded for. Some clear labeling will help avoid any issues.

To edit the metadata for an image, simply click the thumbnail. A new screen will pop up with these fields:

- URL (you can't change this one).
- Title: By default, the title is taken from the file name of your photo. Sometimes that's good enough, but taking some time to reformat it for greater readability doesn't hurt. Feel free to re-name it entirely too.
- Caption: When you insert an image into a WordPress *Post*, *Page*, or *Gallery* you often have an option to include the image's caption. Entering the caption here means you don't have to enter it multiple times later whenever you add an image. Plus, if you ever need to change the caption you can do it in just one place. Exactly where this text will display depends on your theme, but it usually shows up below or next to the image.
- Alt Text: If you've worked with HTML before, you're probably familiar with this one. The alt text is text that appears if a browser is unable to show your image. This is especially important for visually impaired users. Try to make this field a brief description of what can be seen in the image.
- Description: Think of the description as a longer caption. Word-Press gives every image its own *Page* automatically. If a user clicks on your image, by default they'll be taken to that *Page*. There they'll see the image itself and the description. This is very impor-tant for many of the gallery construction methods covered in this chapter.

The difference between a caption and a description for an image can be hard to wrap your head around. I find it helps to think of it in terms of a library catalog. The caption is analogous to the brief record display on a catalog search results page. The description is like the full record— it's what you see when you click through to look at an item's details.

One neat side note: on this edit page there's also an "Edit Image" button on the left side of the page. Clicking that brings up some basic photo editing options like crop and rotate. Very handy for last-minute edits!

Filling out this metadata doesn't take long, but pays huge dividends down the road. Go ahead and invest a few minutes filling it out now, with at least brief information.

Built-in Gallery Options

Recent versions of WordPress have made it much easier to create a great looking image collection. Figure 5.5 shows an example of what you can build out of the box. Holding your mouse over any of those images displays a caption, and clicking on one goes to a *Page* with more details about the image. It's possible to create an attractive and functional basic image gallery without ever installing a single plugin or theme. When you're creating the *Page* you want your gallery to live on, look above the main edit window for a button that says "Add Media."

Click that button to bring up thumbnails of all the images that you uploaded ahead of time. Selecting an image from this screen would insert it individually into your *Page*. That's great, but not what we're looking for here. Instead, look on the left side of the window for the "Create Gallery" link. Click that to switch over into gallery creation mode.

Now creating the gallery is as easy as clicking on the photos you want to include. If you have a bunch of images to scroll through, using the provided search box can be helpful to narrow it down to the ones you want. That time you spent entering image metadata is already paying off!

Now click "Create Gallery" in the lower right corner. You'll see a confirmation with a few options:

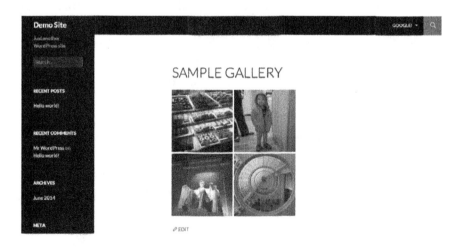

Figure 5.5.   Example Default Image Gallery

- Link To: This drop-down box sets where the thumbnail of each image in your gallery will link to. The default is "Attachment Page." Leaving it set to this option will show users a page with the description you entered previously when they click on an image in the gallery. If you don't have a description or just want to link to the raw media file, change this drop-down to "Media File." Setting it to "None" means the thumbnail won't be a link at all.
- Columns: Pick how many columns of thumbnails will appear in your gallery. If possible, it often looks better to pick a number that can be evenly divided into your number of images. This keeps all of the rows even with each other.
- Random Order: Check this box to randomize the order of the images in your gallery. If you prefer to manually order them, leave it unchecked and drag and drop the thumbnails on this screen to arrange them.
- Type: Thumbnail Grid gives you a grid of small thumbnails. Changing it to Slideshow instead will rotate through one larger image at a time.

Note that your nicely prepared captions also appear below each thumbnail at this point. Once you've tweaked the settings to the way you want them, click the blue "Insert Gallery" button in the bottom right corner.

If you're in the Visual mode of the *Page* editor, you should now see your gallery in the edit box. If you're in the Text view, you'll see an inserted line of code instead. Switch over to Visual if you want to confirm how things look. At this point you can preview, save, or publish your *Page* like any other one you've created. Congratulations on creating a gallery!

If you went with the Thumbnail Grid option, holding your mouse over a thumbnail will show your caption. Clicking on the image will take you to the full page with your full description. If you want to edit your gallery later, go back to the edit view for this *Page*. In the Visual mode, click once anywhere in the gallery. You'll see a small pencil icon appear in the upper left corner, click on that to go back and change any of the options or images you set earlier.

Working With the Slideshow Version of a Gallery

The Slideshow version of a Gallery is what you get if you set the Type drop-down to Slideshow when creating a gallery. This option will show one of your images at a time, rotating through them automatically while displaying each image's caption. While this mode can be useful, it also has some notable limitations.

The size and shape of the slideshow is not easily configurable. It will essentially conform to the largest of your selected images. If one of your images is shorter or narrower than any of the others, it will display with large black bars around the sides. Additionally, clicking on an image in the slideshow does nothing. There is no way to get to the image's individual *Page* from a slideshow, and so no way to see the full Description you so carefully set earlier. If you do want to use a slideshow style display, I recommend looking into one of the slideshow plugins discussed later in this project instead.

Exhibit-Style Themes

WordPress' built-in gallery options are certainly nice, and work well if your exhibit or images are just a part of your larger library website. But what if your site's central purpose is to be an exhibit or gallery? The built-in options can still work for you, but it might also be nice to pick a theme to match your purpose.

Many WordPress themes are explicitly designed to feature images and put less emphasis on text. If you have a good selection of visual material to work with, they can make for a striking introduction to your website.

Believe it or not, the default "Twenty Fourteen" theme included with WordPress has some nice options to feature images on your homepage. With a few settings tweaks, and without writing a single line of code, we can make it look something like figure 5.6.

Here's how to replicate this layout in the Twenty Fourteen theme. First, you need to set one display option:

- Under the "Appearance" section of the WordPress admin menu, click "Customize."
- In the menu on the left, click "Featured Content."

Figure 5.6. Example Exhibit Theme

- Select whether you want your homepage to have a Grid (multiple images displayed at once) or a Slider (one larger image displayed at a time, which users can flip through) layout.
- Click "Save and Publish."

Next, you need to assign content to be featured on your homepage:

- Back in the main black admin menu, go to *Posts* and click "Add New."
- Give your *Post* a relevant title.
- Near the bottom right corner of the page is the Tags box. Add a tag called "featured" (without the quotation marks) to this *Post*.
- Just below the Tags box is a Featured Image box. Click the "Set Featured Image" link.
- Select the image from your media library that you want to display on your homepage. Click the "Set Featured Image Button."
- Publish the *Post*.

Now go take a look at your homepage. Enjoy your new featured slider or grid layout! To add extra images to your homepage, just repeat the steps above. For more information on working with the featured image layout in the Twenty Fourteen theme, the WordPress codex has a very helpful page at http://codex.wordpress.org/Twenty_Fourteen.

Other Exhibit-Style Themes

If the default Twenty Fourteen theme's image options aren't quite what you're looking for to feature your collection, other options certainly exist. I recommend revisiting the WordPress theme directory at http://wordpress.org/themes. Look in particular at the options to filter the directory at http://wordpress.org/themes/tag-filter/.

Under the Subject column one of the filter options is "photoblogging." While a library image collection isn't quite a photoblog, that description is close enough in this case. Look at those themes and see if any of them meet your needs. I'm particularly fond of Phogra (http://wordpress.org/themes/phogra) and SKT Full Width (http://wordpress.org/themes/skt-full-width), but see if any others catch your eye too. If you need help installing or working with themes in general, refer to the previous project in this chapter.

Image-Focused Plugins

If you don't want to make your whole WordPress site heavily image-focused with a theme, but the built-in Gallery options aren't configurable enough for you either, you can always fall back to using an image slider plugin. I mentioned earlier that while the built-in WordPress gallery feature is quite nice, the slider component leaves a bit to be desired. Thankfully there are countless plugins to help you build an attractive and functional image slider into your site. You can see a long list of them at http://wordpress.org/plugins/tags/wordpress-slider. Sorting through them might be a bit daunting, so you can see some of my favorites in figure 5.7.

Metaslider

While Metaslider is a free plugin, that doesn't mean it isn't powerful. While some of the features are locked behind the Pro version of the

Figure 5.7. Example Metaslider Image Gallery

plugin ($19), the free version still lets you create attractive and professional looking image sliders using a straightforward interface and without writing a single line of code. Take a look at what's possible before you try it on their examples page: http://www.metaslider.com/examples. If you want a free image slider plugin, Metaslider is the one to go with.

Slider Pro

I'll admit a bit of bias here, since Slider Pro is the plugin we use for image sliders on http://library.unc.edu. But if you want extremely finely detailed control over your slider, Slider Pro offers every option you could ever want. As a nice advantage, Slider Pro is responsive and will adjust to any device's screen size. Not all sliders have this function. The plugin costs $28 at http://www.sliderpro.net.

Elegant Themes

Elegant Themes isn't just an image slider plugin—a $69 purchase gets you their massive library of professional themes, plugins, and layout options. Their image slider has a preview at http://www.elegantthemes. com/preview/TheProfessional/shortcodes/#imageslider. To my eye, the Elegant Themes image slider's style matches perfectly with the rest of WordPress. If I didn't know better, I'd say it was built into the site itself. The Elegant Themes package is worth looking at for more than

Figure 5.8.   Example SliderPro Image Gallery

just their image slider, but the slider remains a compelling component on its own too.

The Media Library Assistant Plugin

WordPress' default options for organizing your media library are quite good, but sometimes lacking in the details of organization that might come naturally to librarians. Media Library Assistant (https://wordpress. org/plugins/media-library-assistant/) is a plugin designed to help solve exactly this problem, and it does it very well.

While it has many features, the best part about Media Library Assistant is that it lets you organize your media with WordPress' categories and tags. Once you've added this plugin, you can categorize any media you've uploaded in the exact same way you'd handle standard *Pages* and *Posts*.

Media Library Assistant also adds options like bulk editing of image metadata and (if you want to get really detailed) support for common extended image metadata formats like IPTC and EXIF for your images.

If your WordPress site has more than a handful of images, Media Library Assistant is a must-have.

HOW TO ANALYZE AND MANAGE YOUR CONTENT IN WORDPRESS

It's easy to get lost in all the amazing bells and whistles WordPress provides and forget that at its core WordPress is a content management system. All these wonderful plugins and options certainly help manage aspects of your content, and the previous project in this chapter was all about how to manage and use image galleries. But what about the text content that's at the core of most library websites?

Having a well-planned content management strategy is crucial to the success of any website, whether or not it's built in WordPress. But WordPress has many tools available to implement your strategy and make it easy to keep an eye on your content to better meet your users' needs.

You've already learned how to work with *Pages* and *Posts*, and how to organize them with categories and tags. This project will show you how to dig deeper, introducing you to an arsenal of powerful tools and settings that make it simple to keep your site's content fresh and current.

Gathering Usage Statistics

It's difficult to feel informed about the status of your site without statistics to look at. By identifying your most and least popular pages, you can make informed design decisions that improve the usability of your site. For example, if you can see that nobody is clicking on an event registration link, you might consider making it a larger font size or featuring it more prominently on the page. Then you can check the stats again after making the change to see if it improved. Without the ability to pull those usage numbers in the first place, it's very hard to make these kinds of decisions.

The *Google Analytics by Yoast* Plugin

Google Analytics is a free tool made available by Google to track usage of your site. It produces detailed reports on just about any fact you want to know about how your site is used. You can watch how users navigate through your site, what page they usually arrive at, see what browsers or devices they're using, and countless other data points. It's a powerful tool that probably deserves a book of its own. If you're interested in using Google Analytics, I recommend you check out Google's official training materials at http://support.google.com/analytics/answer/4553001.

Setting up Google Analytics involves putting a piece of code on every webpage you want to track. That code will log your visitors' information to look at later. If the code is missing from a page, then you won't get data for any visits there. If you were manually managing a pile of HTML files, you can see how it might be difficult to make sure that code is included on every single page. By using a content management system like WordPress, we can have the system do the work for us. Many plugins exist to handle integrating Google Analytics into your site, but I recommend Google Analytics by Yoast (https://wordpress.org/plugins/google-analytics-for-wordpress/) in particular.

Yoast's plugin simplifies the Analytics setup process to an almost ridiculous level:

- After signing up for a free Google Analytics account at www.analytics.google.com, go into your WordPress admin menus and install and activate this plugin.
- After activation, click the new "Analytics" link in your admin menu.
- Go to the "Settings" section of the plugin.
- Click the "Authenticate With Your Google Account" button.
- Follow the login prompt and allow the plugin to access your Google Analytics account.
- Once you're returned to the WordPress menus, pick your Analytics profile from the dropdown menu.

That's it; no manual setup is necessary, and more importantly there is no need to update the code if Google makes any changes to how their Analytics work. This plugin will handle that problem for you.

Google Analytics will take about a day to start gathering statistics on your site's usage. So go take a break for a while, then come back and start gathering valuable insights into how users are interacting with your site.

The Real-Time section of Google Analytics (see figure 5.9) lets you watch live as users visit and interact with your site.

The Content Drilldown section of Google Analytics (see figure 5.10) shows you how many views each page gets, plus countless details like how they got there, where they went next, and many other statistics. This sample image is just scratching the surface.

Statistics from the Jetpack Plugin

The Jetpack plugin was covered in the first project in this chapter, "How to Install and Use Common Plugins." For information on installing and configuring the plugin, check that section.

Statistics are one component of the plugin and are very useful in analyzing your site's usage. To view them, click on the "Jetpack" menu item in your black admin menu, then click on "Site Stats."

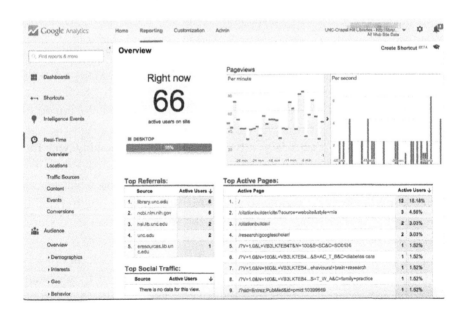

Figure 5.9.   Google Analytics Real-Time Data

Figure 5.10.   Google Analytics Content Drilldown

While not as detailed as the stats you'll get out of Google Analytics, the Jetpack statistics menus are extremely easy to use and understand.

The main site stats menu includes a number of helpful charts and graphs:

- The largest and topmost chart shows you an overview of your site's traffic for the previous days, weeks, and months.
- The Referrers box shows you what other websites have linked to yours.
- Top Posts & Pages is pretty self-explanatory, showing you the most popular content on your site.
- Search Engine Terms make an effort to show you what search terms are leading people to your site, though keep in mind that it isn't always possible to know what the terms a person used were. Still, any data is better than none!
- Clicks shows you what links users clicked on that took them away from your site. For libraries, it might be common to see your catalog or some e-resources listed here. Because they tend to be

hosted on servers separate from a library's main website, analytics packages view them as a separate site.

I want to point out one setting in Jetpack's statistics in particular. At the top of the Site Stats page, click the "Configure" link. Note in particular that you can choose whether to count pageviews of logged in users. By default, Jetpack *excludes* these statistics. This means that all of your pageviews while you build the site as an administrator won't show up in the stats. I'll leave it up to you to decide whether this is a good thing or not. Library employees often don't use a website in the same way your users do, so we may produce significantly different statistical paths through your *Pages* and *Posts*. No method of excluding staff visits to a site is perfect, but using this setting is a good step if that's something you want to do.

Plugins to Assist with Content Analysis and Management

Looking at usage statistics is an important element of making decisions about your website, but they're not the only data relevant to the process. These plugins make it easier to organize or manage your content, and also ease the process of implementing your content-related decisions.

CMS Tree Page View

The CMS Tree Page View plugin (http://wordpress.org/plugins/cms-tree-page-view/) is designed to let you view the structure of your site at a glance.

WordPress' default list of your site's *Pages* is organized primarily alphabetically by *Page* title. It makes an effort to distinguish which *Pages* are children or parents of other *Pages*, but at a glance it can be hard to make sense of all this information in the default WordPress display format. This is particularly true if you have a large number of pages in your site.

Installing this plugin adds a Tree View option to your *Pages* menu. This new view lets you expand and collapse the structure of your site, and makes it very simple to see how your *Pages* relate to each other in the overall structure of your site.

You can even use the Tree View to drag and drop your *Pages* around, reorganizing them into a new hierarchy. *Pages* are also clearly marked as "Draft" when appropriate, making it easy to see which parts of your site are live and which are still under construction. The CMS Tree Page View plugin doesn't change how your WordPress site functions, but it does make it much easier to administer.

Content Audit

The Content Audit plugin (http://wordpress.org/plugins/content-audit/) helps you run a content inventory or review right within WordPress itself.

After any site has been live for a little while, it's a good practice to periodically go back and review it for issues like currency and accuracy. Pick a time period that works well for you, but usually reviewing your pages every six months or annually is just fine. By reviewing your *Pages* you have the opportunity to update them, delete them if they're no longer necessary, rewrite content, or make any other changes that come to mind. Often this process is managed in a large spreadsheet listing all the pages on your site and your notes for each one. This can be a bit cumbersome and error-prone, so why not do it right within WordPress itself?

After installing and activating the Content Audit plugin, each of your *Pages* gets a new option box. It's called Content Audit Attributes, and is visible in the right side column while editing a *Page*.

While the items you see in this box are customizable (under *Pages*, click "Content Audit Attributes" to change them), by default they let you mark a *Page* as Audited, Outdated, Redundant, Review SEO, Review Style, or Trivial. As you go through your *Pages*, simply check off whichever of these attributes apply to each one.

After marking up your *Pages* this way, click "Dashboard" in your admin menu bar and then click "Content Audit Overview." Here you get a simple list of which *Pages* are in each category, plus the option to download the results as a .csv file for easy use in Excel, Google Sheets, or another spreadsheet program. Making decisions about updating or deleting your content has never been easier!

Sort By Modified

Sort By Modified (http://wordpress.org/plugins/sort-by-modified/) is one of my all-time favorite WordPress plugins. It adds a simple feature that I wish WordPress had by default, and does it with no fuss. There's no configuration needed, no confusing options; it just plain works and makes managing WordPress *Pages* even easier.

By default, the main WordPress *Pages* menu lets you view and organize your list of *Pages* by Title, Author, Number of Comments, and Date. Clicking any one of those column header labels lets you easily sort by that column. When it comes time to do a content audit or analysis of your site, it's often useful to know which *Pages* haven't been updated recently. At first glance, you might think that sorting by the Date column would give you an easy way to see that kind of list.

Unfortunately, the Date column contains the date the *Page* was created, not the date it was last updated. Knowing the creation date of a *Page* isn't the data that would be helpful in this case—we want to know when it was last updated instead.

Installing and activating the Sort By Modified plugin adds a new column to that primary *Pages* list: Modified Date. Like the other columns, clicking the label at the top of the column easily sorts by that date.

Thanks to this simple plugin, it's easy to see your oldest content at a glance. Those *Pages* are often ripe targets for a review or revisit.

Managing Other Pieces of Your Site

The content of your site isn't the only thing you need to manage. The previous project in this chapter talked about how to best manage your media library within WordPress, for example. I hope you've picked up by now that with WordPress, if you want to do something there's probably a plugin to help you get the task done. That absolutely holds true in managing your site beyond your simple text content.

Export Users to CSV

It's important to make sure your list of WordPress users is kept up to date. If you're not the only one managing your site, you can easily end up with active accounts for student employees, volunteers, or others who are no longer associated with the library.

Another of my favorite "it does what the names says" plugins is Export Users to CSV (https://wordpress.org/plugins/export-users-to-csv/). Installing and activating this plugin gives you an easy way to download a spreadsheet of all your active WordPress user accounts.

Go to your "Users" admin menu, and click the aptly named "Export to CSV" option. Set the date range to meet your needs, and click "Export." You'll download a nicely formatted CSV file, ready for use in a program like Excel or Google Sheets. Working from this spreadsheet is much easier than copy and pasting information for each user individually out of WordPress' administrative interface.

The spreadsheet itself contains all kinds of info about each account. Personally, what I use the most is the e-mail address column.

Here's an example of how I use the spreadsheet from this plugin. Once a year, I log in and download the CSV file. I copy and paste the e-mail address column into a new e-mail, and send a message to all our current account holders. I ask them to reply if they still need their WordPress account to be active. If I don't hear back, or if the e-mail address returns as invalid, I know to deactivate their account. Limiting site access like this to only those users who truly need it is important for security and maintenance issues.

Tidying Up Your Media Library

It's tempting to leave the Media Library of WordPress alone. It does what it needs to, and the images show up where they should on your site. But what about when you delete an image from a *Page*? That image remains in your Media Library, ready to potentially be used again in another *Page* or *Post*. This might be a good thing, or it could be bad if that image contains outdated info or is from an old site design.

Like most things in life, in this case an ounce of prevention is worth a pound of cure. When you delete an image from a *Page*, or decide not to use it in the first place, take a second to also delete it from your Media Library. This bit of housekeeping is good for your server disk space, good for ongoing management of your site, and good for any other library employees who help manage the site. When they know the only images they see in the Media Library are the ones they can use, it's much simpler for everyone involved to keep your site current and accurate.

Reusing Blocks of Text

While you're using these tools and principles to do a content audit of your WordPress site, keep an eye out for any blocks of text or other content that you reuse across different pages. In any website, not just in WordPress, it's a best practice to not maintain this text in multiple places. It's too easy to let one or more of them get out of sync with the rest, and the next thing you know you've got a minor mess on your hands. Thankfully, WordPress has two tools designed to avoid this problem entirely. Either one will let you maintain a chunk of content in a single copy and display it on multiple pages.

The project about working with Themes earlier in this chapter mentioned widgets as one solution. They're a great option, as long as you want the content in question to appear in a sidebar or footer. If you want it to show up in the main body of a *Page* or *Post*, widgets aren't the best solution. Widgets also assume that you want them to appear on every single *Page* or *Post*, which again might not always be the case. So Widgets are a great feature of WordPress, but they don't solve every reusable content problem.

That's where Shortcodes come in. They're an amazing feature and don't tend to get much attention in WordPress tutorials and articles. The next project will show you how to work with them in-depth to make managing your content even easier.

HOW TO CREATE REUSABLE CHUNKS OF TEXT WITH SHORTCODES

If you spend any time working with the raw HTML view in WordPress *Posts* and *Pages*, you might start to notice bits of text that look something like this: [gallery].

Those bits of text with square brackets around them are one of WordPress' most powerful, and often underused, features: shortcodes. Shortcodes serve as shortcuts for more complicated code or long bits of text. Think of them as placeholders for other pieces of content.

Remember that WordPress is, at its core, a content management system. One of the main advantages of using any system like this is that it obviously will help you manage your content. Websites often have the same information repeated across multiple pages. You might have library hours on every page, or maybe building use policies that appear on pages for multiple branches. If a change gets made to that content in one place, it's easy to forget to make that change in all the other copies too. Shortcodes solve this problem by letting you create your content once, then push it out to multiple pages across your site automatically.

How a Shortcode Works

Here's the basic workflow for creating a library hours shortcode. We'll look at each step in detail later:

1. Create a new shortcode, named "libraryhours" (it's best not to have spaces in a shortcode name).
2. Fill that shortcode with info about your building's hours.
3. Go edit a *Page* where you want your hours to appear. Put this text in the exact spot where you want them to show up: [libraryhours] (including the brackets; they're important).
4. Repeat step 3 on every *Page* where you want your hours to appear.
5. When it's time to update your hours for a holiday or other change, just go edit your shortcode. Any changes that you make there will automatically show up on the *Page* you edited in steps 3 and 4.

Building and Using Your First Shortcode

Earlier in this chapter you learned how to customize your WordPress site using additions like plugins and themes. Both of these things tend to add new features to WordPress, extending it to make it better. Shortcodes are a little different. Believe it or not, this feature is actually built right into WordPress. While in my opinion it doesn't get nearly enough press, anyone can work with shortcodes in WordPress right out of the box. Of course, there's a catch: by default, you need to create and manage your shortcodes via writing code in PHP.

But we can fix that! We'll turn to a plugin after all, one that adds a point and click, user-friendly interface for working with shortcodes.

Installing the ShortCodes UI Plugin

The plugin we're looking for is called ShortCodes UI. Search for that plugin, get it installed, and activate it. If you're new to plugins, check out the first project in this chapter ("How to Install and Use Common Plugins") for the steps to easily get it added to your site.

While there are many plugins designed to make shortcodes easier to work with, this one is my personal favorite. Don't be afraid to experiment with others, but ShortCodes UI is simple and straightforward to use.

Creating a New Shortcode

After activating your plugin, you'll see a new link added to your black admin bar: "Short Codes." Click on that to get to your new shortcode management tools. The first screen you'll see is pretty empty, because you haven't created any shortcodes yet. To fix that, click the "Add New" button near the top of the screen.

Now your screen should look familiar, since the setup is very similar to creating a new *Page* in WordPress. There are lots of optional fields to fill out to customize your shortcode, but there's really only three things you need to fill out:

- The first field at the top of the page says "Enter Shortcode Name." Give it any name that you want. Make it something that you'll understand later, since this is the title that will appear in your master list of shortcodes.
- The main editor box is where you enter the content you want to appear on each *Page*. In our library hours example, this is where you can list the actual hours of your library. You can format it the same way you would any other content in WordPress.
- Scroll down a bit and find the Shortcode Tag field. This is the text you'll put between square brackets everywhere you want your chunk of content to appear. Continuing our example, put library-hours there (with no space between the words and no brackets).

The rest of the fields are completely optional, and get into more advanced shortcode usage. I do want to point out one in particular though, the ShortCode Template box. If the content for your shortcode uses complicated HTML formatting, put it in this box instead of the main editor box above. But for our simple library hours example, you can pretend this one doesn't exist either. Now, just click the blue "Publish" button.

Using a Shortcode in Your Pages

If you know the name of the shortcode you want to use in your *Page*, it's very simple to use. To continue using our library hours example from above, just type [libraryhours] (including the square brackets) in the *Page*'s edit box. Now if you preview or save your *Page*, you'll see your content displayed just as you created it. Repeat the process on a second *Page*, with the same results! You typed that content just once when you set up the shortcode, but can have it published across as many pages as you want on your site.

You might end up working with a large number of shortcodes, and it can get a little difficult to remember the names of each one. In this case, instead of directly typing the square bracket shortcut into your edit box you can select it from a list instead.

While editing a *Page*, put your cursor where you want the shortcode's content to appear. Now look for a button at the top of the window that looks like < > (if you're in the visual editor) or says Short-Codes UI (if you're in the text editor). Both buttons do the exact same thing, so just click whichever one you see.

A window will appear with options to look through all your created shortcodes in a dropdown list. Select the one you want, then click the "Insert Shortcode" button. You should now see the shortcode in your editor box, complete with square brackets. To see the actual content on your *Page*, just click "Preview" or save your changes to the *Page*.

Editing or Updating a Shortcode

This is all great so far: you've learned how to type content into a shortcode just once and publish it on multiple *Pages* across your site. But how can you update that content? Back to our example again, let's assume that your library's hours have changed. Before shortcodes, you would have had to go edit each page individually. Depending on the size of your site, that could be dozens or hundreds of edits to make! And if you missed just one of them, suddenly your site has outdated content.

Instead, just go back to the Short Codes section of your black admin menu bar. Find the shortcode you want to update, and click on the title. Make any changes you want in the edit box, and click the "Update" button.

That's it! The changes you made have been pushed out to every *Page* you used the shortcode on. Congratulations on stepping up to a new, more effective way to manage your common pieces of content.

Other Applications of Shortcodes

Shortcodes are one of my favorite features of WordPress. They make it easy and straightforward to keep complicated structures of content up to date and current for your users. But creative developers have found other ways to use them too.

We've looked at basic shortcode usage here, but they really are an amazingly powerful tool. Many plugins also make use of shortcodes as part of how they work. The Formidable plugin, discussed earlier in this chapter, for example, uses shortcodes to insert your forms into your pages. WordPress' default gallery, also covered in an earlier project, uses shortcodes to insert your image gallery into a *Page*. The Elegant Themes plugin mentioned in an earlier project also includes ways of using shortcodes to format your text into columns, boxes, buttons, and other layout pieces.

Any time you run across something in one of your *Page*'s edit boxes that has text between two square brackets, that's a shortcode. Some shortcodes, like the gallery one, get more complex than just having the name of the shortcode between two brackets. You might see extra bits of text there too. You might see options listed, such as how many images to display in the gallery, or which format to use. But don't worry about exactly how that code is structured—you can pretend that it doesn't exist and trust that WordPress is doing the heavy lifting for you.

Shortcodes are such a powerful feature that I expect their use to expand in the coming years. You're in on the ground floor, ready to see them take off!

HOW TO BUILD A PROFESSIONAL LIBRARY WEBSITE

By now you've got every tool in your arsenal that you could possibly need to create a professional, attractive, and functional library website. No matter what kind of library you work in, the same tools still apply. You might use them in slightly different ways, but they all come from the same toolbox. As a general outline of the process, here's how to best apply them. You can refer back to earlier sections of the book for any refreshers or pointers.

Choose a Type of WordPress

The first decision you should make is whether to use the .org of .com version of WordPress. Refer back to chapter 2 for more information on this choice, but I recommend you use the .org version if at all possible. The expanded customization options it offers are very hard to do without on complex sites.

Pick a Webhost

Assuming that you chose the .org version of WordPress, you'll need to find a place to host it. Talk to your local IT department to see if they have the hardware on hand to run a server, or look elsewhere at the third-party options mentioned in chapter 2. This may be a little tricky if your website has historically been hosted by a central organization which you have little control over. If needed, try walking them through some of the customization options covered in this book. Hopefully they'll see the advantages of working with a robust, mature, and secure content management system like WordPress.

Get a Basic Site Up and Running

Your next goal is to set up a plain, vanilla, uncustomized WordPress site. This is the blank slate you'll build your library's website on. At this point, don't worry about what it will look like or how the content will be organized. You're focusing on the technical fundamentals instead, making sure all the pieces are working together and getting familiar with WordPress. Your IT department may take care of this for you, or if you went with one of the third-party hosting options from chapter 2, then setup is probably just a couple clicks.

Now is the time to get your hands dirty. Because this blank WordPress site isn't your final website yet, this is your chance to play around and get familiar with WordPress. Install some themes, add a plugin or two, and create some dummy *Pages* and *Posts* to work with. Remember that you can delete it all once you're comfortable with how WordPress works, and start again for real. This is a perfect chance to try out different designs and themes, or maybe even mock up a basic homepage to do usability testing with or to show to your administrators. This is your rough draft—putting in a little time now getting familiar with the options and methods covered in this book will turn you into a confident WordPress developer and user in no time at all.

Install and Customize Your Final Theme and Plugins

If you've been playing around with WordPress, now's the time to wipe it clean again. Go delete the themes you tried out but didn't settle on, as well as any plugins you decided not to use after all. If you had some dummy *Pages* and *Posts* set up, get rid of any you don't want to keep for the final version of your site.

Now's the time to revisit the "How to Install and Customize a Theme" project from earlier in this chapter, as well as "How to Install and Use Common Plugins." Remember to set up a child theme to ease any upgrades down the road, and start to hash out what you want your site to look like. As you start to zero in on a theme and organization for your site, it's a great time to show early drafts to your users or patrons. Can they easily find their way to complete common tasks in your design? It's easy enough to make changes at this point in the process if any issues come up. Test early, test often!

Set up Content Analysis Tools

The project in this chapter on "How to Analyze and Manage Your Content" in WordPress introduced you to tools for managing usage statistics, organizing your content and media, and other tips for better WordPress organization. These kinds of tools are much easier to set up now, early in your site's lifetime, than they are later.

Set up the stat gathering tools in particular as early as possible. You can't go back and retroactively gather stats later that you aren't tracking now, so now's your chance to make sure you don't miss anything.

It's also very helpful to establish workflows for managing your content at this point. It's very easy to put this off until later, but figuring out how you'll manage your multimedia content now, for example, will save you the headache of trying to sort through dozens or hundreds of images to find the one you want later.

Once you've got these management and analysis tools in place, it's time to look at your content.

Find Your Reusable Content

Look back at the previous project about shortcodes. Remember how easy it is to set up reusable blocks of content? Pulling content out like this makes it easier to keep up to date later. Take a look at all the content on your old site, pre-WordPress. Do things jump out at you that repeat from page to page?

Maybe your branch hours or building usage policies show up on many *Pages*. Do you have staff contact information that appears in multiple places? Make a list of any content that gets repeated this way, and create a shortcode for each item.

Build Your Pages and Posts

At last, you're ready to start populating WordPress with your content in *Pages* and *Posts*. Your site should be in good shape visually and structurally, so it's time to actually put words into the website. Using the shortcodes and other management tools that you set up earlier, whenever possible you can copy and paste your content from your old site (if you have one) into WordPress. As a side note, this is also a great opportunity to reread all of your website's content and look for issues in voice, tone, spelling, jargon, and so forth that can plague library websites.

Launch and Iterate!

Congratulations! You built a beautiful library website in WordPress. Show it off proudly to the world, but don't forget to come back and keep improving it. There are new WordPress updates, improvements, and plugins all of the time.

REVIEW

In this chapter you got your hands into WordPress' inner workings. You should now feel comfortable configuring and tweaking your site into one that meets your users' needs well.

You learned:

- How to Install and Use Common Plugins
- How to Install and Customize a Theme
- How to Build an Exhibit to Display an Image Collection
- How to Analyze and Manage Your Content in WordPress
- How to Create Re-Usable Chunks of Text With Shortcodes
- How to Build a Professional Library Website

That's an impressive arsenal of tools! You can extensively change how your site functions with plugins, how it looks with a theme, feature beautiful images in your *Pages*, analyze your content for insights about how your site is being used, and build shortcodes to make your content management job easier.

Thanks to these tools, you're ready to work on your library's site. Pick a theme, install some plugins, and get building! The next chapter will point out some tips and tricks to work with along the way.

6

TIPS AND TRICKS

By now you're well on your way to success with WordPress. You know how to get it set up, how to customize the display and add functionality, and how to manage your content inside the system. You have a variety of plugins in your arsenal, and know how to craft a site that meets the needs of your users. This chapter goes just a little bit further, pointing out some tips and tricks that can help keep your WordPress site humming along happily well into the future.

ENHANCING SECURITY

You might read all kinds of doom and gloom about WordPress security issues. While it's certainly an important consideration, it's not nearly as bad as you might fear. Once again an ounce of prevention is worth a pound of cure. Here are a few extra steps and tools that can help you keep your mind at ease.

Sucuri Security

Chapter 5 included a section on how to set up and use the Wordfence security plugin to keep your site safe and secure. It does a great job, but keep in mind that it isn't the only option out there. Other plugins like Sucuri security (http://wordpress.org/plugins/sucuri-scanner) can add an extra line of defense on top of Wordfence.

Moving Your Login Page

Every WordPress site has its login page in the same place: www.yoursite.org/wp-login. If an attacker wants to gain entry to your site, that's the first place they might look. By changing your login page to an address like www.yoursite.org/sitemanagement you add an extra hoop for any attacker to jump through while not terribly inconveniencing yourself.

The easiest way to move your login page to a custom location is, as usual, via a plugin. In this case the plugin, aptly called Move Login (http://wordpress.org/plugins/sf-move-login/), works well.

Keeping Your Site Updated

The simplest thing you can do to keep your site secure is to keep it updated. Each new version of WordPress contains security fixes which help minimize any risks to your site. Luckily, recent versions of WordPress have taken steps to make this process much easier and more transparent.

Minor updates are installed automatically, without any need to configure even a single option. Major updates that include new features or enhancements to WordPress will still require your approval to update. WordPress will tell you when these updates are available. Whenever you log in, keep an eye open for an alert message saying that it's time to upgrade. From there, it's just a couple of clicks to get your site back up to date.

Other Updates

Don't forget that WordPress has other bits and pieces that might need to be updated. WordPress will also alert you about any updates to your plugins. Installing these is simple too—once you see an alert, WordPress will walk you through the process with just a couple of clicks. There's no need to access a FTP or do any code editing.

Themes are the final piece that might have updates available. Like plugins and WordPress itself, you'll get an alert when one is available for a theme you have installed. If you haven't made any customizations to your theme, go ahead and update just like you did with the plugins. Again, it's just a couple of clicks.

If you have made customizations, there's one extra thing to check before you update. The previous chapter included the project "How to Install and Customize a Theme." If you worked through those steps, you should have a child theme up and running that is handling any customizations you made to the theme. If you have that child theme, go ahead and update with the confidence that your customizations will remain intact. But if you've made customizations to your theme's code and didn't use a child theme, updating may overwrite those customizations. Make sure you document what you changed in advance, before updating, so you can remake those customizations easily again afterward.

Backing Up Your Site

It never hurts to have a good backup. Whether you're working with plain HTML files, a full content management system like WordPress, or any digital files at all really, having a good backup is just smart business. And like most tasks in WordPress, you guessed it, there's plugins available to make this process pretty easy.

There's two main things you need to backup from WordPress:

1. your actual PHP and related files from your web server; and
2. your MySQL database.

Like most content management systems, your actual webpage content is stored in a database. The PHP and other files that are on your web server know how to talk to that database and format the data into the version we see on the web. Without the database the PHP won't know what to display, and without the PHP the database is just text without any structure. So we want to make sure we grab both of those. There are two ways to do this.

Backing Up Your Database and Files Separately

Backing up your PHP and related files is pretty easy. Using your FTP program of choice, just log into your web server and download all the files. Put them all in a safe place (and having more than one copy on different computers doesn't hurt) and remember how to get to them.

Make sure to update your backup with current versions after any major changes or updates to your site.

Getting a copy of your database would be a little trickier if we didn't have a good plugin ready to do the work for us. Install the WP-DB-Backup plugin (http://wordpress.org/plugins/wp-db-backup) for the task. If you need help installing plugins, refer back to the plugins section of chapter 5. There are many database backup plugins to pick from, but I've used this one for years and have had a good experience with it.

After installation, look in the "Tools" section of your black admin menu. There's now a new "Backup" link—click on that. You'll see a few options of how to back up your database. It's best to include all of the tables, and then just pick how you want to save the resulting backup. I recommend having it both e-mailed to yourself and saving a down-loaded copy onto your computer.

Down at the bottom of the backup options, you can even configure the plugin to automatically e-mail you a database backup every so often. I highly recommend setting this up. The backup files are small and don't take up much space, so there's no harm in having them arrive frequently.

Again, put a copy of your files and database in a safe place. On the off chance that you ever have a major issue with the site, these can be used to get everything back up and running quickly.

Backing Up Your Database and Files All At Once

While it isn't free, the BackupBuddy (http://ithemes.com/purchase/backupbuddy) plugin makes backing up both your files and database dead simple. It includes elaborate backup and restore options, includ-ing the ability to save your backups to cloud storage services like Drop-box. Plans start at $80 per year, which is a small price to pay for peace of mind. Their website has a great overview of how the plugin works, summarizing all of the features in an easy to understand way. If you don't want to back up your database and files yourself as discussed above, BackupBuddy is a great option.

If you've followed all these tips, your site is both more secure from attacks and more secure from any accidental hardware failures. It never hurts to be prepared!

WORKING BEHIND THE SCENES

When doing web work, it's common to work on new pages or features in private where the public can't see them. These in-development pages aren't quite ready for public consumption, and sometimes you'll want a way to keep them hidden for a bit. WordPress has a number of ways to accomplish this goal.

Moving between Servers with BackupBuddy

The BackupBuddy plugin discussed previously can, with a little creativity, help you move from a development site to a live one. In this setup, you'd have two WordPress sites running. One is your live, public site, and the other is a private site that only you know how to get to. You can do whatever you want on the private site without fear of the public seeing it before it's ready.

When it's time to move your site from the private site to the public version, simply have BackupBuddy installed on both sites. Use it to back up your private site, and then restore it on the public site. Now you can work safely in private until your new *Pages* or other content are ready for their big debut.

If you do want to use BackupBuddy to move content between test and live installations of WordPress, you might want to look into running your test version on your own computer instead of on a web server. This is a more complicated process to set up, but there are links to more information in the Recommended Reading section.

Working with Private Pages

If BackupBuddy is out of your price range or you don't have the resources to run an extra WordPress development site, private *Pages* are good alternatives.

Every WordPress *Page* has a visibility option. It can be set three ways:

1. *Public*: Anybody on the web can see the *Page*.
2. *Password Protected*: Users are prompted for a password before they can see the *Page*.

3. *Private*: The *Page* is only viewable if the visitor is logged into WordPress. If they're not logged in, they can't access the *Page*. To someone not logged in, it will look like the page doesn't exist.

To change a *Page*'s visibility setting, look in the "Publish" box near the upper right corner of the edit screen. Click on the blue "Edit" link next to the eyeball icon to see the available options (see figure 6.1).

Setting a *Page* as password protected might seem like a good option to hide it while you build the *Page*. But this provides a potentially annoying experience to site visitors. It advertises that a *Page* is there, but they're not allowed to see it.

Making a *Page* Private while it's in development is a better idea. This way any library staff with a WordPress account can log in and see the *Page*, but to anyone else it will look like it doesn't exist. When your *Page* is ready for the public, simply switch the visibility setting to Public. There's no need to use any plugins or do a full backup and restore process between sites.

Setting *Pages* as private during development is the quickest and easiest way to develop your content without releasing them to the world in the process.

SMALLER TWEAKS

These are some of my favorite small WordPress plugins. Most of them do very simple things, but all of them greatly enhance my use of Word-Press every day.

Broken Link Checker

Sometimes a plugin's name tells you exactly what you need to know about it. The Broken Link Checker looks at all the links on your site and e-mails you whenever it finds a broken one.

The plugin is very configurable, letting you specify what portions of your site it should search and which types of links it should ignore. In an ideal world we wouldn't have any broken links to begin with, but every now and then one slips in. It's very useful to get the alerts and be able to fix them on the spot.

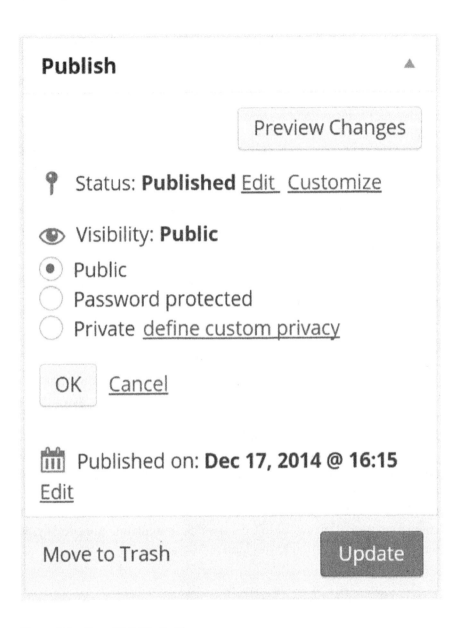

Figure 6.1. Page Visibility Settings

Disable Comments

While WordPress lets you disable comments on an individual *Page* or *Post* (see chapter 3), by default it doesn't have an option to turn them off all at once. If you have more than a handful of *Pages* on your site, going through and toggling comments off for each one becomes a bit of a task.

After installation of a plugin called Disable Comments, you'll see a section for it under your WordPress settings. There you can switch off comments for everything on your site, just *Pages*, *Posts*, Media, or any combination of the three. If you want to have comments disabled on all but a handful of your locations on your site, that's easy enough: Use this plugin to disable everything, then go back and individually re-enable the ones you want to keep.

The option to have comments in WordPress is great, but it can become overwhelming to maintain on a large site. It's also a matter of opinion whether having old comments on a page make it look outdated or not. Additionally, not every page lends itself to comments. Sometimes a prominent link to a feedback form or e-mail address can serve just as well. This plugin gives you that flexibility.

WordPress PopUp

The WordPress PopUp plugin adds options to display a popup message on your homepage. Have you ever used website where you saw a message asking you to take a survey or provide feedback? WordPress PopUp makes it easy to configure and launch one of your own.

There are options to control which pages the popup appears on, how often a user will see it, avoid showing it on mobile devices, and many more. I have used this to recruit users for usability testing campaigns on the UNC libraries' website. I was initially worried that the popup might annoy our users, but we didn't get a single complaint. Anecdotally, it seems that users are used to this kind of interaction.

Active Directory Integration

Does your organization already have a login system that uses Active Directory? That might be your institutional e-mail accounts or some other login. If so, this plugin lets employees use that same login on your WordPress site.

While WordPress can happily maintain its own accounts, the passwords for those accounts won't be synced up with the passwords employees use for other work-related tasks. If your organization uses Active Directory, this plugin ties the two together and keeps the passwords in sync. This is more a matter of convenience than anything that actually impacts the functionality of your site, but sometimes convenience is worth a little bit of extra effort.

As another advantage, you're still able to create WordPress accounts outside of your Active Directory structure. You aren't locked into using Active Directory logins alone with this plugin.

Social Media Integration via Jetpack

The Jetpack plugin was covered in depth in chapter 5. It adds so many features to WordPress that it was impossible to cover them all there. Two of my favorite smaller features are that it adds easy ways to display your library's Facebook and Twitter widgets in your site's footer or elsewhere.

The process for adding them will vary slightly depending on which theme you've chosen, but in general:

1. Go to the "Appearance" section of your menu, find your theme, and click the "Customize" button
2. Click on the "Widgets" section of the customization menu
3. Click on which area of your theme you want the widgets to display in. This might be a sidebar or footer, for example.
4. Click the "Add a Widget" button.
5. Click either the "Twitter Timeline (Jetpack)" or "Facebook Like Box (Jetpack)" option.
6. Configure the widget with your information, then click the "Save & Publish" button at the top of the screen.

That's it! Your site now has dynamic widgets for your library's Facebook and Twitter presences.

WordPress Multisite

This is a more complicated tweak, but is a good one to be aware of. By making a simple change to one file in WordPress, you can turn your site into a WordPress Multisite version.

By default, WordPress runs just one website per installation. But in recent versions it became possible to host multiple sites under one installation. This version is what powers WordPress.com, for example. Each administrator can have access to and control over their own WordPress site, completely walled off from others running on the same server.

Why might you want to do this?

- To run a site where users can create their own WordPress blogs.
- You're part of a very large organization, and different departments want to have their own WordPress site completely under their own control.
- Your library wants to run a traditional website on WordPress while still having separate WordPress-powered blogs for various projects and departments.

The details of working with the multisite version of WordPress are beyond the scope of this book. But like all WordPress features and functions, it's well documented online. Visit the WordPress Codex at http://codex.wordpress.org/Create_A_Network for more information.

7

FUTURE TRENDS

WordPress has a bright future. Since its initial release in 2003, this little content management system has grown into something massive. But what does that continued growth mean? What can we expect to see in it going forward? Because WordPress is an open source project, there isn't one spokesperson or company who can entirely lay out a vision or roadmap. But we do have the next best thing: Automattic.

Founded in 2005, Automattic is the company that runs Word-Press.com. Remember that this service is the free version of Word-Press. Automattic hosts the site for you, and you get limited customization options for free. So they obviously have a vested interest in the future of WordPress too. Once a year, Automattic's founder Matt Mullenweg gives his "State of the Word" address. As one of the guiding forces behind WordPress' advancement, this speech is always worth listening to. His latest speech was given at the end of October 2014, and is available online at http://ma.tt/2014/10/sotw-2014/.

This speech outlines some fascinating statistics and paths forward:

- WordPress powers 23.3 percent of the web, up from 17.4 percent in 2012. If that growth rate continues, WordPress will be even more important in the future than it is now.
- 2014 was the first year when non-English downloads of Word-Press surpassed the English downloads. Expect a ton more Word-Press usage, plugins, and contributions from new places around the world.

- Accordingly, Mullenweg noted that in the near future WordPress development will focus on internationalization. Expect more pieces of the interface and WordPress-related tools like the plugin and theme directories to be more fully translated.
- There's also a focus on the WordPress mobile apps going forward. These apps focus on publishing to your site from mobile devices, so I'm not sure they have much relevance to the way most libraries edit our sites. But still, it's worth keeping an eye on.
- Mullenweg gave an early preview of a WordPress REST API. Defining what this is could get fairly technical, but it has the potential to enable much closer integration of WordPress with other services. Imagine being able to easily embed a WordPress *Post* or *Page* in any web page anywhere, whether it's powered by WordPress or not, and you get some idea of what this might do. A few years from now we may be able to much more tightly integrate WordPress portions of library websites with our catalogs and other content management systems.

WordPress is here to stay. With this level of adoption across the web and such strong signs of advanced feature development going forward, I have no qualms telling libraries (or anyone else) to build their site in WordPress. The community is here, and it's not going anywhere.

RECOMMENDED READING

BOOKS

Goodman, A. L. (2014). *The comparative guide to WordPress in libraries: A LITA guide.* Chicago: ALA TechSource. Amanda Goodman's guide to is an excellent resource for implementing WordPress for your library and configuring the features to best serve your library's users.

Hedengren, T. D. (2014). *Smashing WordPress: Beyond the blog* (4th ed.). Chichester, West Sussex: Wiley. Smashing WordPress goes in-depth on some of the more technical aspects of WordPress. If you're interested in advanced customization options and not afraid of writing a little code, this is the book for you.

Jones, K. M. (2013). *Learning from libraries that use WordPress: Content management system best practices and case studies.* Chicago: American Library Association. With chapters written by different librarians who have each implemented WordPress in their own libraries, this book goes in-depth on some practical WordPress-related projects.

Etches, A., & Schmidt, A. (2014). *Useful, usable, desirable: Applying user experience design to your library* (1st ed.). Chicago: ALA Editions. While not specifically about WordPress, Amanda Etches and Aaron Schmidt's guide to user experience design in libraries should be required reading for any librarian or library staff member who works on the web. Many of its lessons are directly applicable to designing sites in Wordpress.

WEBSITES

There are so many websites about WordPress out there that it's hard to narrow down a list enough to fit in this book. But these are my very favorites: the resources I find myself turning to over and over again.

http://codex.wordpress.org. The WordPress Codex is your number one resource for Word-Press documentation and troubleshooting. Whether you need help installing, upgrading, working with a theme, working with plugins, or pretty much anything else, the codex has help for you.

http://codex.wordpress.org/Installing_WordPress_Locally_on_Your_Mac_With_MAMP. This particular page of the Codex outlines how to set up a copy of WordPress that runs on your own Mac instead of a server somewhere else. While nobody else can see your site this way, it does give you a way to experiment with building a WordPress site in private.

http://codex.wordpress.org/Installing_WordPress#Local_Installation_Instructions. These instructions provide PC-compatible options for running a WordPress site on your own computer.

http://developer.wordpress.org. Wordpress's Developer Resources has an extensive guide for developing your own plugins. It will soon have an equally large section devoted to custom theme work. Lastly, you can dive deep into WordPress' underlying code here.

http://wordpress.org/support. If you're stuck with a question and the Codex doesn't have what you need, your next stop is this WordPress support page. It will walk you through some common troubleshooting, plus you have the option to post a question in the support forums. The WordPress community is very friendly, and someone will usually try and help you out quickly. If you've ever tried Googling a question about WordPress, you probably ended up on a post in these forums with an answer.

http://lib20.pbworks.com/w/page/59677899/WordPress-Libraries-examples. Polly-Alida Farrington maintains this extensive list of libraries of all types that use WordPress. Browsing them can be a great source of inspiration and ideas for building your own WordPress site.

http://guides.masslibsystem.org/content.php?pid=313714&sid=2890517. Another list of libraries using WordPress, this list is also very useful for ideas and inspiration.

http://Lynda.com. While not free, Lynda's broad array of online technology training courses includes more than sixty courses related to WordPress. They range from quick one-minute video introductions, to a feature, all the way up to six-hour walkthroughs and overviews.

http://www.wordpress.tv. Automattic runs periodic conferences for WordPress developers called WordCamps. If you can't go in person, the videos of sessions are posted later on this site.

INDEX

ABOUT THE AUTHOR

Chad Haefele is the emerging technologies librarian at University of North Carolina Chapel Hill. As part of the User Experience Department he explores evaluation and improvement of the campus libraries' web presence and other points of interaction with users. His areas of research interest include web development, usability testing, personal information management, ebooks, mobile devices, gaming in education, and location-based services. His (WordPress-powered) blog is at www.HiddenPeanuts.com.

Haefele has over a decade of experience with WordPress as a content management system, and he recently worked as part of a team to move the UNC libraries' website at www.library.unc.edu into WordPress. He now works to maintain and enhance the site on a daily basis.

Haefele was named a Mover & Shaker by *Library Journal* in 2011, and he is hopelessly addicted to his iPad and smartphone.